DAVID HASLAM

GO, SELL

An investigation
into the failure
of the British Churches
to meet the
moral challenge of
investment in
apartheid

EPWORTH PRESS

First published 1975
by Epworth Press

7162 0246 8

Enquiries should be addressed to
The Methodist Publishing House
Wellington Road
Wimbledon
London SW19 8EU
Printed in Great Britain by
Clifford Frost Ltd
Lyon Road, Windsor Avenue
Wimbledon
London SW19 2SE

For
Polly, Sara and Dominic
who were also exploited
in order that this book
could be written

CONTENTS

Prologue 1

1 'I see blood and destruction . . .' 3

2 Down on the farm 9

3 Bees in the Company bonnet 17

4 A worm's-eye view 25

5 Of elephants and jaguars 31

6 The owls and the pussycats 49

7 Chicken or fox? 57

Epilogue 60

Prologue

DURING 1974 the map of southern Africa underwent radical change. At the beginning of the year its five dominions of white supremacy, Angola, Mozambique, 'Rhodesia', 'South West Africa' and the Republic of South Africa had appeared solid fortresses of impregnable racialism, whereas by the end the Portuguese colonies of Angola and Mozambique had achieved promises of independence, and white-controlled Rhodesia and South West Africa appeared distinctly unsound. Only South Africa remains apparently untouched, and some say she has already decided to withdraw from the embarrassing commitments beyond her borders, in order to safeguard her own 'white Christian civilization'. For readers who have noted the inverted commas round 'Rhodesia' and 'South West Africa', this is to denote countries which are in transition from white to black rule. The names used by Africans are 'Zimbabwe' and 'Namibia' respectively, and it is these names that we shall use throughout this book.

The Portuguese, who had continued to regard Mozambique and Angola merely as appendages of metropolitan Portugal until late 1973, were by late 1974 assisting both towards an impecunious independence. In the aftermath of the military coup in Portugal, political groups in the colonies which used to be described in the Western press as 'terrorist' began to be treated as the legitimate representatives of their people. During 1975 Frelimo became the accepted government of Mozambique, a similar arrangement is possible with the Angolan liberation groups, and in Zimbabwe there is unwilling and grudging recognition that the African National Council does represent the opinions of almost the entire African people. In Namibia too there are signs of change, though South African Prime Minister John Vorster still seems bent on creating as divided and reactionary a regime as possible in a 'free' Namibia. The extent of 'freedom' which South Africa plans for Namibia will be a matter of considerable debate in the next few years. But, all in all, has not change come at last to southern Africa? Have not the whites now seen the error of their ways, and can we not sit back and watch majority rule flower and multiracial democracy bloom in what until now has seemed to be such infertile soil?

There are two factors to take into account before attempting to answer these questions. The first is that Mozambique and Angola have been liberated only after a decade of wars fought by their respective Liberation Movements, and that such Movements have also been active inside and outside Namibia and Zimbabwe for several years. The second is that although Zimbabwe, Angola and the others are important areas of

European and North American investment, none of them have the immense importance of South Africa. And if they can be sacrificed, while the boundaries of racial supremacy around South Africa hold firm, then their expenditure in the interests of white Western capitalism may have been worthwhile.

Mr Vorster at the end of 1974 once again asked for time. 'Give us six months', he has said. 'and you will see real and lasting changes.' At the same time he has been holding 40 detainees without trial, mostly younger people involved in the Black Consciousness movement which he has sworn to destroy. By mid-1975 Vorster had had his six months, and there has been no fundamental changes in South African society. The present strategy is to take the world's attention away from South Africa, while indulging in the long-drawn-out process of casting 'South West Africa' and Ian Smith's 'Rhodesia' to the African winds of change.

The most frightening thing at the present time is the willingness of leaders in the West, news editors, churchmen, politicians, businessmen, to believe that Mr Vorster really intends sharing power with black South Africans. They should be reminded that Africans today may not work where they like, live where they like, meet how they like, travel when they like, love whom they like. And there is at present no sign of any of these freedoms being just around the corner. Said Cosmas Desmond, author of *The Discarded People,* in a *Guardian* interview of January 1975, 'The most Vorster will do is to give a veneer of decency to the system by increasing black wages, although in fact the black-white wage gap is still widening in absolute terms. There is no sign of ordinary white attitudes changing at all, which is what really matters. The essence of apartheid — white economic and racial supremacy at all costs — remains, and while peripheral things like wages might be getting better, (apartheid) is getting more subtle, more dangerous and much worse'.

What then is the right stance for companies and their investors to take with regard to investment in South Africa? It is the purpose of this book to demonstrate that ultimately the only position that Christians can advocate is that of withdrawal for the company, and disinvestment by the investor if the company in which he invests insists on maintaining its involvement in apartheid in South Africa.

1 'I see blood and destruction . . .'[1]

The historical background

TO UNDERSTAND more fully the variations between the countries and peoples of southern Africa, and the extent of European responsibility for the present state of affairs, some small historical introduction is necessary.

(a) The plunder of the land

The first European settlers in South Africa arrived in 1652. They landed at Table Bay on the Cape, to establish a supply base for the Dutch East India Company. The local African population then consisted of the Khoi people, the so-called Hottentots and Bushmen. A Swedish traveller, who visited the area in the 1720s, remarked that they seldom furnished themselves with weapons, and that their habitations were as plain as their dress. Their society was simple and equal, and this contributed not a little to the happy and peaceful lifestyle enjoyed by these supposedly primitive people. The first Dutch settlers were followed by French Huguenot refugees, then more Dutch and German Calvinists. Their ideology seems to have ensured a consciousness of racial superiority from the start, and the ensuing loss of land, dignity and identity, along with the European diseases brought by the white men, led to a sad and rapid decline among the local tribes.

In other parts of what we now call South Africa the Khoi had already come under pressure from other Bantu peoples, themselves migrating southwards from Central Africa. These more warlike tribes met with the Boers. as the settlers had become known, around the year 1780, as the latter pushed east and north towards the zones of higher rainfall. Battles fought mainly by the Xhosa people waged for some years across the Great Fish River; they were in a way the first wars of African liberation in southern Africa. Later the British also did battle with the Xhosa, and overall it was century before their will to resist was broken.

British power in the area had grown and in 1806 they took over control from the Dutch. Soon they began to exercise this power, and to give some political rights to Africans. Unable to accept this, in the 1820s the Boers began their Great Trek east, bringing them eventually into contact with the Zulu people. The Great Trek ended at the Battle of Blood River on 16th December, 1838, a date still celebrated by the Afrikaaners as the 'Day of the Covenant' when God gave them their 'promised land'. The explorer David Livingstone, who visited the area in the 1840s, was very critical of the way the Boers treated their captured Africans. They were made to do all the agricultural labour and at the same time somehow support themselves and their families.

---

[1]A line from 'Jesus Christ Superstar'.

'I have myself been an eye-witness of the Boers coming to a village and, according to their usual custom, demanding 20 or 30 women to weed their gardens, and I have seen these women proceed to the scene of unrequited toil, carrying their own food on their heads, their children on their backs and the instruments of labour on their shoulders . . . Mr. Potgeiter (a Boer leader) lauded his own humanity and justice . . . "we make the people work for us in consideration of allowing them to live in our country".'[2]

The second half of the nineteenth century developed into a three-cornered struggle between the Boers, the Africans and the British. African rebellions continued in the areas of Namibia and Zimbabwe into the first decade of this century, and it is therefore less than 70 years since the first phase of the African struggle for independence ended. The modern history of southern Africa began with blood and destruction. These have continued to be the dominating factors in the second phase of African liberation which began within a decade with the formation of the African National Congress in 1912.

The Boers were finally brought to heel by the British in 1902, but they were very quickly granted autonomy in the Orange Free State and the Transvaal. So anxious were the British to placate them that they failed to insist on the enfranchising of Africans, mixed race 'Coloureds', or the Asians who had been brought in to work on the railways and in the mines. When the negotiations for the Union of the four provinces in South Africa took place, only in the Cape were there any African or Coloured voters, and when the actual Union came about in 1910 all but a handful of those elected to the legislature were not native to the country but were families of settlers from thousands of miles away. Thus was South Africa born in injustice.

As a post-script it may be worth repeating what by now must have become obvious, that the early trials and tribulations of southern Africa were due almost entirely to the desire for *land*. The whole Cape may once have been 'empty', as white South Africans claim, but the first arrivals were the Khoi, pushed down into the south by other migrating Bantu peoples. The latter were already occupying the north-east when the settlers arrived. It is not without reason that the false myth of the original emptiness of South Africa is still propagated today in South African history books and information literature. White South Africans seem unable to accept that the people now their miners and waiters, their tea-boys and domestic servants, once actually owned the land the whites now live on. The myth of appropriation they can cope with, the truth of robbery with violence they cannot.

(b) Consolidation

More recent history has seen a continual widening of the racial division

---

[2] Basil Davidson, *The African Past*, Penguin, p. 294.

between white settlers of English and Dutch extraction. Each have had their own political parties, and the period between 1910 and 1948 was one of an ongoing struggle for ascendancy. Various coalitions were formed, but on the extreme right the Nationalists steadily increased their support until in the election of 1948 they won a narrow victory. A future of permanent struggle to maintain and perfect the ideology of white supremacy was sealed. The European races found themselves in conflict even over their style of Christianity. The British were mainly Methodist or Anglican, but the Afrikaaners came from the Calvinist Dutch Reformed tradition. The place of religion in the culture of the Afrikaaners, and their 'chosen people' mentality, should not be overlooked as a powerful factor in the ideology of white racialism. Thus political power in contemporary South Africa is firmly in the hands of the Nationalists, the party of the Afrikaaners, though some people of English extraction support the National Party, as some more liberal Afrikaaners support the United Party opposition. Until more recent times the English-speaking population had much more economic power than the Afrikaaners. They used it however just as little to advance the cause of the Africans as the Afrikaans people have done with their political power. Whatever their internal differences white South Africans have combined to block black African advancement.

(c) The drive for liberation

Let us then examine briefly the development of the liberation struggle, first in South Africa itself, then in the other countries of the region. The recognition by the Africans that the first phase of African resistance had been defeated came earliest in South Africa itself, and led to the formation in 1912 of the African National Congress (ANC). At a meeting in Bloemfontein there gathered representatives of most of the major peoples in the Union, and the first stage in the formation of African unity was completed with a statement declaring that Africans were above tribal animosity and were to be One People. The new grouping had its first test in 1913, when the Land Act was passed by the white Parliament, reserving only 13 per cent of the land for the African population. When the ANC sent a delegation to Britain to protest the British government pleaded problems of war in Europe, and thus laid up for future generations decades of political and military struggle in southern Africa. After the European war the ANC again protested, this time about the handing over of what was then German South-West Africa to South Africa, but the European powers were unmoved. Ever since those times the leaders of all sectors of Western society, politicians, businessmen, traders and churchmen have retained an uncanny ability to ignore what the African peoples have said, and to rely on the whites' judgement on what is best for southern Africa.

In the 1920s and 1930s the ANC continued its efforts in the industrial and political spheres, endeavouring to help organize black workers and to protest against the final removal of the vote from the Africans and

Coloureds of the Cape. During the second Northern Hemisphere War (another example of our European arrogance is referring to all our inter-tribal struggles as 'World Wars') there was a renewed upsurge of concern and activity among blacks throughout Africa, and in 1943 the ANC Youth League was formed. This pressed the older generation of the ANC to produce what became the 1949 Programme of Action, including boycotts, passive resistance and strikes. In 1950 there were May-Day strikes, and over the next few years persistent campaigns against Labour Conditions, the Pass Laws, 'Bantu' education, and the whole paraphernalia of the developing apartheid state. Finally in 1955, after a nation-wide campaign for 'Freedom Demands' from the people, the 'Freedom Charter' was launched.

It was enough. In 1956 the South African police arrested 156 members of the ANC and using the Freedom Charter charged them with high treason. Despite all the repressive action, the ANC continued to organize bus boycotts, strikes and anti-Pass campaigns. The culmination of this programme of passive resistance came in 1960 at Sharpeville, when 69 unarmed Africans, including women and children, were killed when police opened fire on a peaceful demonstration. Following this the ANC felt it could no longer urge non-violence on its supporters. Before being forced into violent action, a process brilliantly outlined by Nelson Mandela at the Rivonia treason trials, the ANC had patiently exhausted all the tactics of non-violent opposition. But faced with the system of massive and inhuman violence against their people it is difficult to know what else the African nationalists could do in southern Africa except turn first to sabotage, and then to armed struggle. Chief Lutuli, then President of the ANC ,had called in the early 1960s for an international economic boycott as a last hope of non-violent change. It was ignored by the Western powers, who have continued to ignore the Liberation Movements ever since. They have been forced underground inside South Africa, and if the future of the country does develop into war and bloodshed one group who will not be able to wash the stains from their hands are the nations of Europe, and Britain in particular.

The history of Namibia (South-West Africa) is similarly one of settler expansion spattered with acts of brutal aggression against the indigenous population. In the late nineteenth century the Germans began to extend their control and rebellions by the local people were put down hard and forcefully. Massacres were not unknown, and by 1907 all resistance had ceased. One of the main tribes, the Herero, had been reduced from a rich tribe of 80,000 to a bunch of hungry fugitives numbering no more than 15,000. In 1914 the South Africans invaded the German territory under Smuts and took it over in the name of freedom and justice. After the war' the newly-formed League of Nations decided that Namibia should become a Trust territory of South Africa. Foreseeably the South Africans used their mandate to extend and entrench the system of land appropriation and racial segregation. Over the years Namibia was gradually and irresistibly turned into an extension of apartheid.

When the United Nations was formed, South Africa refused to submit a Trusteeship Agreement for Namibia, and the issue was taken to the International Court. The Court found that South Africa was not legally bound to place Namibia under UN control, she has therefore continued to administer the territory for the past 30 years. Over all that time the International Court has consistently failed to take sufficiently seriously the situation of African oppression.

The contemporary phase of the liberation struggle in Namibia began in the 1950s, and two movements were formed, the South West Africa People's Organisation (SWAPO) and the National Union (SWANU), the former being much the larger. They have both suffered the same problems of organization and mobilization owing to the insuperable obstacles placed in their way by the South African government. It was only in 1966 however, when it became clear that the International Court would not take seriously the Namibian peoples' case, that SWAPO announced reluctantly it could no longer operate entirely non-violently. Like others of the southern Africa liberation movements there is a strong Christian contingent, and they have found it very difficult to take up a stance which is against both their natural inclination and their faith.

As far as Zimbabwe is concerned its links with South Africa extend back to the earliest incursions by the whites, at the end of the last century. Then Cecil Rhodes, Prime Minister of the Cape Province, began the move north to fulfil his vision of a British sphere of influence from the Cape to the Mediterranean. The local Africans again fought their first wars of liberation with courage and some success, but by 1908 all resistence had ceased. Again the ventures of the Europeans were only a thinly-disguised search for wealth and land, orchestrated by the British South Africa Company. No interest was taken in the welfare, education or medical care of the population, except by the missionaries, and it may be argued that their greater gentleness merely aimed at a colonialism of the spirit, rather than the body and mind. In 1923 the British government offered the 40,000 settlers a choice of union with South Africa, or direct rule from London. The Africans were not consulted. Direct rule was the choice made, but in actual fact the settlers have always been left with a fairly free hand to govern themselves. Thus the 1965 rebellion, or so-called' 'Declaration of Independence', did not change the country's affairs excessively. The whites continued to exploit their position of power, and to allow the Africans only minimal improvement. Between 1959 and 1962 most black leaders had been banned, imprisoned, or exiled. Soon the Zimbabwe African People's Union (ZAPU) was formed, although there was some dissension and a group broke away to form the National Union (ZANU). Since then these two groups have co-ordinated most of the African resistance both inside and outside the country, and now co-operate under the umbrella of the African National

Council, formed when the Pearce Commission went to canvass African political opinion in 1972.

A review of the histories of the old Portuguese territories of Angola and Mozambique tells a similar tale of massacre, expropriation and greed. The achievements of the liberation struggles in Angola and Mozambique, and the continuing efforts of the African peoples of Namibia, Zimbabwe and South Africa are essentially a response, a response to the continuing persistent and determined exploitation of their lands and resources which has gone on for the last 400 years. The first aim of the white man was land, but this has now broadened into the pillaging of mineral resources, copper, gold, uranium and diamonds. The positive results for the African population have been few and far between. Claims have been made regarding 'education', 'medical care', 'employment' and the various other 'free gifts' of colonial Western society, but these make a derisory picture compared with the cheap labour, the plundered resources, the expropriated profits and the lush standard of living of most white people in southern Africa. However, whatever the arguments over the past, and whether or not it would have been better had the white man never come, the vast majority of Africans have decided about their future. They demand the freedom to determine their own style of life as nations and the methods by which they will distribute increases in their national wealth. Blood and destruction has been the dreadful legacy of the white predators in southern Africa. It will be a long time before it is forgotten.

2 Down on the farm

Foreign investment and labour control

(a) Harvesting the golden eggs

BY NOW it is well-known that almost every major British company has a greater or lesser investment in apartheid, either through subsidiary companies, or part-ownership of companies based within South Africa. The Anti-Apartheid Movement has published a list of nearly 600 companies so involved. The main source of the 'conscientisation' of the British public on this matter was the *Guardian* revelations of 1973 and the debate which has gone on since, though of course much of the content of the 'revelations' had been known to anti-apartheid workers for some time. Perhaps as much of a shock to the British 'man-in-the-street' as the information about wages and conditions of African workers was the discovery that so many household names were implicated. It had quickly become clear that British industry and commerce was tied up with the exploitation and oppression of apartheid to a degree that few people realized.

How Britain became so deeply enmeshed in the apartheid economy is a matter for international economists. Suffice it to say that our current large stake in apartheid is a considerable embarrassment to many people in this country. South Africa is one of the most profitable areas of investment in the world, and every man, woman and child in Britain maintains their standard of living to some degree through the exploitation of the black workers of South Africa. The interest rate for investments in the region never fell below 10 per cent between 1960 and 1968, and in 1964 reached almost 15 per cent. The Americans did even better, averaging 18.6 per cent between 1960 and 1970[1]. The reason for this high rate of return is of course the cheap, non-unionised, highly-controlled workforce which fulfils all the dreams of most company management. For the ordinary working person there are other drawbacks too apart from the moral one. When wages rise in this country big manufacturers seek other sites for production, where labour is cheaper and the politics are 'stable'. That is why Spain has been a haven for car manufacturers, similarly Portugal for textile manufacture before the coup. That is why most of our chief firms are to be found in South Africa, so much so that British Leyland was in 1974 talking about doubling its investment in South Africa while threatening to shut up shop in this country. The multinational company able to expand in southern Africa can be in a very fortunate position.

Some figures on trade are essential, though we cannot go into international economics in depth. In 1970 total foreign investment in South Africa amounted to around £3,000m of which Britain's share was £1,730m,

---

[1]*The South African Connection*, First Steele & Gurney, pp.30-1

or 58 per cent of the total. The Labour Party review of investment estimated our total stake topped £2,000m by 1973. Western European countries hold about a quarter of the total also, and the United States most of the rest. The Japanese interest is growing, but it remains a small proportion of the whole.

The only period of time in the last 30 years during which foreign investment has not continued to increase was in 1960 when, at the time of the Sharpeville massacre, international confidence in South Africa wavered considerably. £48m left the country that year, but the most powerful international companies held firm, and in some cases increased their investment, thus assisting the South African government through a worrying time. From 1965 confidence recovered, and South Africa received nearly £1,000m in investment between 1965 and 1970 (source, the South African Reserve Bank). By 1971 the annual inflow had reached £447m and was continuing to rise. There is a great commercial interest in southern Africa, and part of that interest is centred on maintaining the *status quo* there. In the last analysis foreign investment and multinational companies are not going to be the force to change the system in southern Africa. They may be prepared to accept minor reforms, but they are much more anxious to keep the situation just as it is.

Traditionally it has been the gold-mines which have been most profitable for foreign capital, and returns of 30 per cent have not been unusual. Wages have been very low, around £2 per week until the recent outcry, but not much better now. In real terms, wages of African gold-miners are the same as or below the value in 1889; for a full account of how one company operates in this field see the Anti-Report on 'Consolidated Goldfields', by Counter-Information Services. British interests in manufacturing in South Africa are also considerable. The biggest examples are ICI's large share in South Africa's second largest industrial concern, African Explosives and Chemical Industries, British Leyland's share in Leyland South Africa, and Associated British Foods' in Premier Milling. Of the country's one hundred leading industrial companies, twenty-five are partially-owned by British Corporations and twelve are direct subsidiaries of British companies. There is thus even just in the gold and manufacturing industries vast opportunity for British business to affect South Africa's philosophy of 'separate development', and there has been for decades. That nothing substantial has happened is due far less to the ignorance about South African conditions than to the plain unwillingness to interfere in any way with a goose which lays such golden eggs. British firms will complain that the misery of apartheid is the responsibility of the government and nothing to do with them. Some will say they are doing what they can behind the scenes to ameliorate the worse excesses of the system. But there has been no attempt to mobilize the potentially enormous power of foreign companies in South Africa to put pressure on the government to institute even the most minor of changes. There have been a few squawks about the lack of skilled labour, though there is often nothing to prevent Africans being given much more training than at present. The extent of actual job reservation is very small, but firms prefer to co-operate with the government, even in spheres where they could bring about some change, in order not to prevent the bringing home of such juicy and delicious bacon.

As well as blaming the government for the lack of change, companies also blame their subsidiaries. They claim to have little or no control over what their subsidiary companies do, but no doubt if profits declined and returns diminished, a way of rectifying the situation would rapidly be found. It may only be concluded that as long as the money rolls in, the methods are considered immaterial.

One more sign of British companies' unwillingness actually to threaten apartheid can frequently be seen in the job advertisement columns of the press. Potential job-seekers, engineers, managers, electricians, accountants are enticed by offers of high wages, delightful conditions, and generous expenses if they will come to work in 'sunny South Africa'. After the *Guardian* articles of 1973 the Anti-Apartheid Movement suggested several ways in which companies could begin to make reparation; one was the training and promotion of African workers, rather than the importing of skilled workers from abroad. British unions have supported this suggestion, and the British Council of Churches added its weight with a report on 'Emigration to South Africa'. If companies really wanted to improve opportunities for Africans they could shelve some of their plans for growth for a year or two while training Africans, and Coloureds or Asians, for more senior positions at all levels. In a celebrated court case involving the *New York Times* American newspapers were forbidden by law to accept job adverts which infer racial selection in the choice of candidates, which all South African jobs do. British newspapers continue to accept advertisements for jobs in South Africa and British companies continue to place people there.

Another valuable area of co-operation for South Africa with Britain is that of trade. Britain receives nearly 30 per cent of South African exports, while South Africa receives only 4 per cent of ours. She still benefits from the system of trading preferences developed for 'poor' members of the Commonwealth, despite having resigned 13 years ago. The food and wine, metals and raw materials which South Africa exports help to pay for the vital imports of higher-technology goods. Therefore once again, by our trade, we assist South Africa to survive in her present form, and have failed to use our considerable influence to better the lot of African workers. There has been much heated argument about the effect of a trade boycott of South Africa. Much of the heat has been generated by those making most money out of the trade.

As for the position of the Africans, it is a long time since Chief Lutuli of the ANC called for an international trade boycott of his country. He said Africans were prepared to suffer for their freedom, and to forgo any improvement in their standard of living, already tragically low in many areas. Western interests however were not prepared to lose their profits for the sake of African freedom. Thus we were told that these leaders did not speak for the majority of the people, it being a well-known phenomenon in the West that people are never prepared to suffer for anything as abstract as 'freedom'. The fact that the white-minority government was not prepared to allow Africans to vote for the political party they supported speaks for itself. It is likely that, given the chance, up to 90 per cent of Africans would have voted then, as now, for the African National Congress, or related groups with similar aims, such as the Pan-Africanist Congress (PAC).

Further exploration of British commercial ties with South Africa is unnecessary. Deeper study could begin with *The South African Connection.* Suffice it to say that the only views and statements allowed to escape from South Africa are those which do not mention economic sanctions. Some of these statements are admittedly from Africans, for there are no doubt a number of Africans in leadership positions in the present system who believe that increased investment may be their salvation. The fact that the South African government has banned, imprisoned or otherwise silenced all the leading spokesmen for the alternative point of view suggests that these are the views of which they are really afraid, because these are the ideas which, if implemented, could be the most threatening of all.

(b) Fencing in the geese

If British business had decided it was going to challenge the conditions of labour under apartheid what kind of problems would it have had to tackle? Low wages of course are the most obvious iniquity, and this was quite clearly recognized when rises of 50 per cent. and 100 per cent. for African workers were announced during 1973. White workers have also been receiving increases however, and 20 per cent. of £50 per week comes to exactly double a 100 per cent. increase on £5 per week. The other insidious force to be fought has of course been inflation. In six months during 1973 the Institute of Planning Research of Port Elizabeth calculated that the cost of living for Africans had risen by 17 per cent. Thus wage increases of 34 per cent. per year are needed just to keep pace with the African cost of living. The Institute examined the records of ten British controlled firms over the same period, and discovered average annual increases of 30 per cent. This was despite the fact that pressure was being created both by industrial unrest in South Africa and by publicity in Britain.

The largest single blockage to international economic justice in South Africa is however the legislation which prevents the official formation and recognition of African trade unions. The Africans have shown themselves to be perfectly capable of negotiating agreements when given the opportunity. If British business really wished to help it would recognize unofficial African unions immediately, and press the government to change the law. In fact fledgling African unions are usually subjected to a good deal of harrassment, and their leaders sacked where possible. For example, in August 1973 most of the African employees at Leyland's Durban plant were members of the black Metal and Allied Workers Union, and they sought recognition from the management. This was refused. Eventually the workers went on strike, and all the 250 strikers were sacked. A few days later most were re-engaged, but a little later on 65 Africans were laid off, including some with 8-10 years service, who were known to be officials of the MAWU.

It is the Urban Areas Act which governs the distribution of Africans in the towns and cities. It tends to cut across the needs of business however by refusing to allow sufficient Africans to reside near enough to their work. It controls the influx of Africans into the urban districts, sets aside areas for their accommodation, and imposes strict control on their movements. The African's residential rights depend on his employment, if he loses his job he and his family can be in serious trouble. This is yet another reason why African labour is cheap and uncomplaining.

A further example of the way these laws work is provided by the migratory labour system. The migrants come from African reserves, or 'Home-lands', and neighbouring countries like Botswana, Malawi and Mozambique. Many of the workers are not allowed to have their families with them, but must live in single-sex hostels for the eleven months they are on contract. It is often cheaper for companies to import labour than to accept the additional responsibility of a worker's wife and children. The migrants come because, though the wages are poor, at home there is no employment at all. The South African economy feeds on their lack of opportunity.

The labour laws are another complex area which would need to be tackled in any effort to relax the constrictions of apartheid. They control the making of wage agreements, and provide for the registration of unions, for collective bargaining and arbitration, and for job reservation. The African is not regarded as an 'employee' and is therefore denied trade union and bargaining rights. He is dependent on white workers to make his agreements, and he may be prosecuted if he fails to abide by them. No investigation can take place over a wage complaint if there is a collective bargaining agreement in force, but as these are the occasions on which an African might wish to file a complaint he is unlikely to be much encouraged.

African workers are of course denied the right to strike. They face four times the penalty which whites do for engaging in illegal strikes, and any kind of organizing to bring pressure to bear over working conditions is likely to lead to trouble for Africans. The 'Suppression of Communism' Act includes in its definition of communism anyone who tries to bring about 'political, industrial, economic or social change by the promotion of disturbance or disorder'. This law was used to arrest 200 African bus workers who in 1961 struck for the same benefits as white and Coloured workers. Some were arrested again on the same charges four years afterwards.

The Bantu 'Settlements of Disputes' Act was designed to take out of African hands for good and all any responsibility for collective bargaining. It provides for State officials to act on behalf of Africans. The sort of situation to which this leads was demonstrated not long ago in the steel industry negotiations. The 65,000 white and Coloured workers were represented by a 120-strong negotiating team, while the 200,000 Africans' interests were in the hands of two government officials. Unemployment benefit is of course an unheard-of luxury to most African workers. In 1950 the Nationalist government excluded all Africans then earning less than £182 per year, which left only 10 per cent. eligible. This legislation also means there is no unemployment register. In 1969 the government estimated there were 80,000 Africans out of work, but in 1971 Professor Sadie of Stellenbosch University calculated a figure of 1.3m, or nearly 20 per cent. of the total work-force.

Accident benefit and industrial injury compensation are of course rarely claimed and even more rarely paid out. The African has usually returned to whence he came before the cash arrives. African workers are without representation, without organization, without protection, and without any of the other employment rights which we accept as the only way of ordering a society based on capitalism. We may not like the capitalist system, but we can force it to operate under a mask of humanity. In South Africa the mask is off, and the exploitation practised by capitalism without constraint is plain for all to see.

As far as the actual wages paid to African workers are concerned it may be useful to add a note on the Poverty Datum Level (PDL) and the Minimum Effective Level (MEL), before considering the minimal responsibilities of the companies, as we do in the next chapter. The PDL is based on the unavoidable expenses every family has to face — food, fuel, clothing, rent, transport to work. The figure for differing areas is different; for an urban area like Johannesburg it has been calculated by groups like the Chamber of Commerce and the Institue for Planning Research. The average arrived at for March 1973 amounted to 76 rand (about £43) per month. The PDL however excludes furniture, cooking equipment, bedding, medical and educational expenses, etc. To add these to the PDL, bringing it up to the MEL, means an increase of 50 per cent, bringing the required minimum wage in March 1973 to £65. With necessary additions for inflation the figure for Johannesburg is likely to rise to £90 in 1975. There is however no provision in this figure for 'luxuries', i.e. travel, stationery, sport, tobacco, sweets, cinema, etc. Taking all things into consideration an average African family would be denied a decent human existence in today's world with less than £100 per month income, and no company's minimum wage should be below that figure. There is as much chance of that happening at the present time as of the South African government passing a law requiring proportional racial representation of senior management, i.e. 70 per cent. African. No, there is a common interest between foreign companies, the government, and the white trade unions, in maintaining the industrial scene in South Africa just as it is. Ever-tightening enclosure of the geese however may at some point cause an explosive dash for freedom which will destroy all future possibilities of a continuing supply of golden eggs. What is more, the farm may become an extremely unpleasant place in which to live.

3 Bees in the Company bonnet

How British business supports apartheid

WHEN the first results of reporter Adam Raphael's investigations in South Africa were published in the *Guardian* on 12th March 1973, the telephone lines between Britain and South Africa began to hum. The number of claims, counter-claims, and immediate clandestine wage-rises, provide a fascinating study of big business, not just with ants in its pants but a couple of bees up each trouser leg as well. Executives and company chairmen overnight became experts in South African wage rates, costs of living, sickness benefit and native lore; 'the African seems to think if he gets an increase he can just sit back and let productivity go to ruin', was a comment by Air Commodore Freddy Rump, Director of UKSATA (United Kingdom-South Africa Trade Association), quoted by Raphael on the same day. Other pre-industrial revolution quotes included one from Mr. Peter Noble, personnel manager for Leyland South Africa: 'I personally am anti-press, I have too much trouble with you lot buggering up labour relations.' Raphael's conclusions were that 'not a single British company employing substantial numbers of Africans is paying all its workers at the humane level of the MEL', then around £14 per week. Many paid very much less, Slater Walker, Tate and Lyle, Portland Cement were all paying wages of less than £3 per week, and Metal Box, Courtaulds, GEC and British Leyland were not much better. A large number of the families of workers employed by British companies were actually in danger of starving to death. But instead of a wave of self-recrimination and acceptance of responsibility the air was filled only with disclaiming voices full of injured innocence.

Eventually the public outcry following the *Guardian* disclosures led to a House of Commons sub-committee being appointed to examine the wages and conditions of South African workers employed by British companies and their subsidiaries. In some ways it was a fruitless exercise in that the committee had no judicial power, but most companies submitted evidence, and some were also cross-questioned by the committee. A lot of murky facts became public knowledge, but after two years they are in danger of being forgotten. One of the main groups on whom lies the responsibility for remembering is the shareholders of these companies. Up to now it seems to have been the responsibility only of share-holders to put their money into a company; now the movement for 'Corporate Responsibility' has led to a situation where this is not sufficient. Not only should corporations become more responsible to the society in which they exist, but large investing groups such as churches, universities, local authorities and charitable foundations should also take an interest in the sources of their income.

Otherwise the situation develops where the National Society for the Prevention of Cruelty to Children, or the Church Missionary Society, may be receiving dividends from companies who by their activities and wage-rates are actually causing the conditions which they are trying to ameliorate. Or again the Church of England General Synod, having passed a resolution expressing abhorrence of racialism, finds that a substantial proportion of the Church's income is derived from exploiting weaker racial groups. It may be that companies' 'Corporate Responsibility' is only enabling the capitalist system to adjust the mask under which it works; it may also be that this is one way in which the underlying philosophy of capitalism may be exposed.

The evidence to the Trade and Industry sub-committee of the House of Commons' Expenditure Committee which investigated the wages and conditions of African workers covers four large volumes and over 1,600 pages of print. A total of 37 witnesses or groups of witnesses gave evidence, 32 of them representing companies or commercial businesses, and over 100 other companies responded with written evidence. Firms were often represented by their Chairmen, and sometimes brought in special witnesses from South Africa. The Committee made it clear from the beginning that their investigation was not into South African government policy, and that there was no implication of the committee being a Court of Law. They stated they were merely assembling evidence, and that their interest was confined to the activities of British companies and their subsidiaries, to the extent that this country should be responsible for the activities of business organizations which are based within its shores. This line of reasoning set the committee's effectiveness at the rather low level of publicity, and gave the lie to the assumption that automatic improvements would follow the committee's report.

A summary of the evidence submitted by fifty companies has been produced by Christian Concern for Southern Africa, entitled 'British Companies in South Africa'. It may however be useful to summarize briefly the evidence given by three companies who appeared before the Commons sub-committee. We choose British Leyland, General Electric Company and Rio Tinto Zinc, not because they are any worse than anyone else, but because they are fairly typical, and they represent a cross-section of British manufacturing and mining interests in that country.

(a) British Leyland

Ninety per cent. of Leyland's Coloured workers in their Capetown factories (43 per cent. of all employees) were in 1973 paid a monthly basic wage 17 per cent. below the PDL for Coloured workers in that area. Where black workers could get up to semi-skilled wage levels they earned only a third of what their white counter-parts did. Fringe benefits such as pensions and medical care decreased down the scale so that the workers who were worst off and in greatest need received the lowest benefits. At Leyland's

Annual General Meeting in London at the beginning of March 1973, Lord Stokes, the Chairman, stated that the company's African employees were among the best-paid in South Africa, though a week later a company spokesman admitted that its wages were in fact lower than other motor manufacturers such as Ford, General Motors and Chrysler. (the *Guardian* 13th March 1973). In fact a 30 per cent. increase was granted to the lowest-paid workers in April 1973, the month after the *Guardian* revelations, and Lord Stokes first claimed in evidence to the Trade and Industry sub-committee that this was the result of a pay review begun in the previous May. 'It simply became obvious that the cost of living was escalating at a greater rate than the wages we were paying' ('Evidence', Vol. 1, p.139). The fact that it took 11 months to find this out was not commented upon by Lord Stokes. Nine months after the *Guardian* findings Leyland were still paying a minimum black wage of 19 rand per week, against the Minimum Effective Level of around 27 rand (*Johannesburg Financial Mail,* December 1973). The Sub-committee Evidence made clear that the main pressure for increasing wages was African strikes and British public opinion. Left to themselves the company might not have increased African wages to this day. The problem of African advancement was raised with the Leyland management by the committee, and it was pointed out that as there were no African apprentices at all in Leyland South Africa, African workers were unlikely to rise too high up the promotional scale. Management replied that white workers would not accept Coloured or Black apprentices. 'This is an understanding we have with the unions there', said Lord Stokes, Leyland's chairman. When pressed as to whether there was any legal agreement he said, 'I do not think it has been put in such forceful terms as that because it is the general practice and custom of the country'.[2] Here we have a clear example of where a British company, possibly acting with others, might have considerably improved the opportunities of African workers, but was prepared to sit back and let injustice roll on for the sake of a quiet life, and satisfactory profits.

(b) The General Electric Company (GEC)

GEC is one of the largest British employers in South Africa with a labour force of over 7,000. It was another of the companies which mysteriously gave a rise to its lowest-paid workers in April 1973, 15 per cent. to those in the bottom bracket which brought them above the PDL, but only by working a 50-hour week. Before this 25 per cent. of the work-force were paid below the poverty line for the basic 45-hour week. 51 per cent of the company's employees are Africans, but they receive only 22 per cent. of the total wage bill. The Company rejected in its evidence any responsibility to pay above the PDL for a family in the given area of its operations, though since then it has given undertakings to raise all basic wages above the MEL.

[2]*Minutes of the Expenditure Committee* (Trade and Industry sub-committee), Vol. 1, p.143.

In response to a question by the author at the Annual General Meeting in August 1974 the Chairman of GEC, Lord Nelson of Stafford, stated that it was now company policy to raise wages above the MEL for a basic 45-hour week within two years, i.e. from the publication of the Commons sub-committee report. In its evidence to the committee the company claimed that any rapid increase in wage rates might affect its ability to continue its South African operations. The implication was that white workers might refuse to accept them, and thus the bogey of white strike action was raised to excuse the company from paying African workers a living wage.

When asked what system of negotiating the company followed with its African workers, the reply was 'it is not a matter of negotiation, we do not negotiate with Africans as such'. When pressed as to whether the white unions took Africans into account when bargaining the response was evasive. 'The question of timing is all-important in what one does in the wage structure. In the last 12 months for example, there has been a conditioning process, perhaps, where the higher grades have been prepared to see an uplift in rates of pay for Africans without this having any very serious effect on differentials.'[3] Thus white workers might accept slightly higher wages for black ones, as long as they retain their vastly higher standards of living. There is certainly little hope for economic justice in South Africa through the white unions.

GEC has consistently refused to give information on its profits from its operations in southern Africa. It says that this is not company policy anywhere in the world. The conclusions we are led to draw however are that profits are too high to be publicised without considerable embarrassment, and that the company could well afford to pay higher wages while continuing to make a reasonable profit. The kind of mentality by which British management still approaches the South African situation was summed up in an answer by Lord Nelson at the same August 1974 A.G.M., in response to a question as to why Africans had to work between 5 and 10 hours overtime to pick up a living wage. He said, 'Africans don't mind working overtime, in fact they enjoy it'. That such statements could still be repeated 18 months after the *Guardian* reports demonstrated that British industry still has a long way to go to disentangle itself from the feeling that workers should always be paid the minimum that can be got away with. In fact it may be seriously doubted as to whether such a fundamental re-adjustment in attitude can take place at all.

(c) Rio Tinto Zinc

One of the most contentious areas of employment in southern Africa is mining; the wages that are paid, the profits made, and the conditions under which the workers have to operate. Rio Tinto, the multinational mining corporation, has some of its most profitable operations in southern Africa,

---

[3]Ibid., p. 182

the chief one at present being the enormous copper mine at Palabora, where over 2,000 Africans are employed. The evidence of the company management to the Trade and Industry sub-committee in 1973 showed that white wages averaged nearly five times the Africans' wage, and that two-thirds of the latter earned less than 65 rand (£37) per month, well below even the PDL. The company claimed that as the PDL had not been properly calculated for the Palabora district, it could not be said to pay below it. Later, when the company determined the PDL despite protests that only the MEL should be calculated anyway, it turned out to be lower than other similar districts. The company is now stated to have raised all wages above the poverty line, and to have ensured a minimum rate of £44 per month, but this is still well below the MEL. One figure not quoted in the sub-committee evidence was that in 1970 43 per cent. of RTZ's world profits came from Palabora, even though the mine is a comparatively small slice of the Corporation's global interests. One figure that was quoted however was the 6 per cent. of costs which went on African wages, compared to the 48 per cent. coming home as profits. When Sir Val Duncan, the RTZ chairman, was asked if African wages could not have doubled without having any real effect on profits he had to agree. When asked the reason he replied, 'It is difficult to dissociate yourself from the community in which you are operating in your general decisions. Indeed it must be so because we obey the law whatever it is.' Mr Joel Barnett M.P., a committee member, queried. 'But is there no law to prevent you increasing your African wages?', Sir Val answered; 'None whatever.'[4] It may further be argued that if the customs, or more particularly the law, of a country requires one group of workers to be paid less than another because of the colour of their skin, then the company should not be operating in that country at all.

The recommendations of the sub-committee included a suggested 'Code of Practice' for British companies with interests in southern Africa. It begins with the somewhat vain hope that the companies 'would recognise their own interest in establishing a name as good employers, in particular by keeping abreast of the best current practices and opportunities for advancement'. The record so far however suggests the only way this will happen is by constant and persistent public surveillance. Otherwise companies will subside into the semi-darkness in which they were operating before March 1973. The Code points out that companies have considerable power in the fields of wages, fringe benefits, training and promotion opportunities, even within the South African legal system. It is unlikely however that sufficiently powerful pressure will be forthcoming from British shareholders to achieve this. It would be more constructive in the long run to support the recognition of African trades unions, and such groups as SACTU, the banned South African Congress of Trades Unions, the ANC and PAC. Only they represent the fundamental change necessary.

---

[4]Ibid, p.249.

The Code of Practice suggests that in the absence of trade unions 'Works Committees' should be established, though these should be only a stage on the way. There is no law to prevent the recognition of African trade unions, though only a handful of British companies seem prepared to recognize them. The Code continues with various suggestions as to how the companies can improve the lot of their workers, but as the committee as a whole failed to tackle the basic question of the re-distribution of power, the Code's ideas are merely reformist in tone. There is nothing intrinsically wrong with them, but with all the ballyhoo that surrounded the sub-committee, we might have hoped for something a little more hard-hitting. In fact the South African government were reported as being fairly satisfied with the tone of the report, so it quite clearly contains no real threat to the apartheid system.

In December 1974 the government followed up its sub-committee report with a White Paper which suggested among other things that companies should give information on wages and employment practices in South Africa in their Company Reports. The MEL for the region in which they were operating should be stated, and a timetable for achieving the payment of a decent living wage to all employees. Companies were also encouraged to report on what they were doing to meet the government's 'Code of Practice' on African advancement and trade union rights. Information however was to be given entirely voluntarily, and the Paper stated that only 250 of the 600 British Companies operating in South Africa had replied to a letter on the subject by Peter Shore, the Secretary for Trade. A number of companies were quoted in the *Guardian* as refusing to commit themselves to the government's request, and this response pointed once again to the value of informed and persistent questions at a Company Meeting, which is the only forum where management can be called publicly to account. If a company has disclosed material it can be questioned upon it, if not it can be asked very pointedly why. After the initially poor response Mr Shore followed up his request with a strongly-worded demand that information should be published, and hinting that legislation might be introduced if it were not forthcoming. There is still much work to be done however in ensuring that all information is made available, and then exposing it for its reformist nature, if that is indeed the situation.

There can be no doubt that the revelations about the conditions of African workers have been extremely embarrassing to the South African government, even though the regime's basic policy remains unchanged. Information may not be come by so easily in the future. The South African government has now taken steps to curb the flow of reports on wages, conditions and restraints of labour. The General Law Amendment Bill of late 1974 now makes it an offence to provide information about the operations of local companies which are wholly or partly foreign-owned. The law was created largely to ease American pressure on executives of

De Beers Mining Corporation to give details of their mining and selling operations. However it could have a wider application. Asked if the Law could be used to prevent the gathering of facts by foreign governments about labour conditions the Ministry of Economic Affairs replied that it could. Thus such information may only be given if the Minister gives approval.[5] The passing of this quite minor law symbolizes the real situation in South Africa, which is that the government has no intention of allowing foreign companies to make more than minor alterations in their policies. If any really fundamental change is contemplated the law will step in. None of the companies has in fact tested this out yet, none of them, either individually or in concert with other firms, has challenged any part of the oppressive system by which the white minority controls the country. Big business merely reacts to pressure put upon it; it will not create such pressure unless it believes it is within its own self-interest to do so. And that is not a very satisfactory basis for action, as the low level of activity since the House of Commons Report has shown. Large companies do not want unions, they do not want to give their employees fringe benefits, they do not want to lose a labour system which provides labour as required, they do not want to pay their workers more than the minimum possible wage. As we have seen, multinational companies cannot be seen as a force for radical social change in southern Africa, the sort of change that will create African majority rule. In fact the reverse is the case. When the chips are really down, as after Sharpeville in 1960, big business will rally to the support and the defence of the white minority regime.

We have no objection to the reform of the system, i.e. raising wages, improving conditions, operating training schemes, etc. It must however be recognized that this will not create real change in South Africa. The argument must therefore be taken a step further as to whether foreign companies involved in southern Africa should be asked to withdraw until they can do business there with some semblance of humanity and justice. The African position on this matter is examined in the next chapter, but the crucial point to understand is that companies cannot be expected even to raise wages on their own volition, never mind consider withdrawing from South Africa. They will have to be put under very considerable pressure to take seriously the possibility of acting on moral or ethical, rather than on commercial, criteria. A couple of bees, even Department of Trade and Industry ones, will not be enough. The situation requiries much harsher and more effective agents of change. A swarm of hornets, rather than somewhat aimless bumble bees, conjures up a more realistic vision. Hornets are well-known for producing rapid and urgent action by those upon whom they concentrate their attention. On the issue of South African investments hornets may well be an ideal model for the Church.

---

[5] *Johannesburg Financial Mail*, 18th October, 1974

4 A worm's-eye view

The African position

WITHIN the countries of Africa, Asia and Latin America there has been in the last few years a growing doubt about the whole concept of 'development' and what is meant by it. This is not the place to discuss fully the thinking behind this unease, but it is a fact that such leaders as President Nyerere of Tanzania and Archbishop Helder Camara of Recife in north-eastern Brazil have become spokesmen for a philosophy which suggests that dependence on overseas grants and loans may be a dangerous process of sinking into debt, and that foreign investment may be one of the most powerful forces preventing real independence from Western control. Camara for instance attacks vigorously the low prices paid by the rich for raw materials, compared to the high ones they charge for their own products. He denounces the immense power concentrated in the hands of the multi-national companies, and exposes how these supposedly 'competitive' giants combine together to destroy anyone who has the temerity to challenge them. Chile is one of the examples, and how President Allende was destroyed. In an interview in the *New Internationalist* in 1972 Camara asserts' 'We Christians are not political revolutionaries or extremists, but we cannot be satisfied with charity, or minimal reform. Where there is injustice it must be removed. This will inevitably mean great changes in both developed and developing worlds'.

This is part of the thinking that is challenging the West's traditional views of growth and development. It applies to southern Africa too, and has been an influence on the philosophies of the Liberation Movements. Eduardo Mondlane, the first President of Frelimo, wrote in a book published in 1969, the year he was assassinated, about the 'economics of exploitation', and explained how the Portuguese had held on to their overseas provinces so long because they were a source for raw materials and a market for home-produced goods. The Portuguese had also eliminated all restrictions on the entry of foreign capital to the colonies, thus gaining financial and economic support for the maintenance of the Portuguese empire. Then Western companies who had investments in the colonies would, if a colony's status was in danger, put pressure on their government to assist. Hence the tacit support of NATO which Portugal enjoyed during the decade of its colonial wars in Africa, and the total distrust of foreign investments by the African Liberation Movements.

This short digression into the question of foreign investment in other situations somewhat different from those of South Africa nevertheless gives us important insights into the correct attitude towards foreign investment.

The fact that the Liberation Movements in what used to be the Portuguese colonies have consistently argued for withdrawal of such investment shows what store the Africans have set upon the subsequent loss of confidence which withdrawal would cause among those in power, and upon the spirit of self-reliance it would generate among the local people. The involvement of multinational banks and construction companies is attacked in a Report to the World Council of Churches' Commission on Development by the Front for the Liberation of Mozambique (Frelimo). In Mozambique the most outstanding example of this was the Cabora Bassa Dam, on the Zambesi River. Vast loans were made available by international finance houses to the Portuguese government and to the French, Italian and German contractors (the British and the Swedes withdrew under pressure). There was a campaign in Britain against Barclays Bank as one of the financial underwriters of the dam and this campaign still rumbles on. Cabora Bassa was intended to supply power to a large area of Mozambique, but also to South Africa. Hence it had the political support of many Western governments. Now the dam 'belongs' to Frelimo it is something of an embarrassment. It can only be made economic by supplying power to South Africa, and this Frelimo has no desire to do. Arguably Cabora Bassa is more of a hindrance than an asset. It is a symbol of how Western interests and foreign investment can distort a country's development and curtail its freedom.

All the southern Africa Liberation Movements have at some time made statements condemning foreign investment, and asking for it to be withdrawn. There can be no doubt that among those committed to the liberation of Namibia, Zimbabwe and South Africa there is complete agreement as to the damaging effects of such investment, and the psychological support it gives to white-minority governments. Both ZAPU and ZANU, the two original Movements in Zimbabwe, made their position clear in statements to the United Nations in 1973. George Silundika, the Information Officer of ZAPU, said to the Special UN Committee on Decolonisation, in support of the U.N.'s own position, 'The United Nations action in our support is in trying to break down the economic citadel of the Rhodesian racist regime. We all know that the basic problem in this line of action is the fact that all those countries who have prevailing economic interests in Rhodesia operating through various corporations and related trading partners are not prepared to act in support of sanctions against Rhodesia. In fact they are doing everything possible to strengthen the economy of the Rhodesian regime, undermine the resolutions of the UN on this question, and frustrate the Zimbabwe liberation struggle. The United States of America, West Germany, France, Japan and Italy, and the related satellites, are the main factors in this international conspiracy against African liberation and independence.'[1]

On the same day, before the same UN Committee, Mr S. V. Mtambanengwe, Secretary for Political Affairs of ZANU, pointed out that

[1]*The Struggle Against Colonialism in Southern Africa,* UN publication, p.14.

the limitations of the committee's work were the direct consequence of British hypocrisy in Rhodesia. 'British, American, French and Japanese economic, colonial interests trampling underfoot and riding roughshod over the peoples of these colonial countries in order to exploit the rich oil fields of Angola, the rich gold mines of South Africa, and the rich chrome, tobacco and asbestos of Rhodesia . . . are the real "niggers in the woodpile", to use that odious expression."[2] Mr M. M. Mudzi, then ZANU's Executive Secretary, went on to call for strongly-enforced international trade sanctions on Rhodesia, to isolate completely the racist regimes in Rhodesia and southern Africa. 'We appeal to the United Nations to impose sanctions on all southern Africa covering the entire coast-line of Africa south of Zaire in the west and Tanzania in the east, and to condemn the USA for its importation of Rhodesian chrome and France, West Germany and Japan for breaking the present system of UN sanctions'.[3] Such stringency is not now necessary since the coastlines of Angola and Mozambique are now free.

As far as Namibia is concerned both tribal leaders and the leaders of SWAPO have made statements condemning foreign investment. Chief Clemens Kapuuo of the Hereros has been one of the most outspoken critics. 'We wish all foreign firms to be removed immediately; we wish to be consulted on ways and means by which our people can have a fairer share in benefiting from the land of their birth. This country, which is our country, is being exploited by greedy entrepreneurs, robbed of its wealth, and rendered barren for the future. Our fear is that when freedom finally comes to this land it will be returned to us with no minerals left.' There can be no clearer statement of the conditions under which foreign firms might invest in Namibia. They may be invited to do so when the South African presence has been removed, but until then they should leave the country's resources until such a time as their development may be controlled by the legitimate representatives of the people.

The United Nations has had a special interest in Namibia since its inception. It took over the mandate for the territory from the old League of Nations and since then has been engaged in trying to release South Africa's grip on the country. As far as international support is concerned the problem has been the same as that with Zimbabwe, that the powerful countries of the West, with their economic interests in Namibia, have pursued a policy of liberal public statements along with minimal economic action. Resolution 283 (1970) of the UN Security Council formally adopted the UN's position on Namibia, including a call to all States to withhold from companies of their nationality 'government loans, credit guarantees, and other forms of financial support that would be used to facilitate trade or commerce with Namibia', and further to ensure that 'Companies and other commercial and industrial enterprises owned by or under direct control of the State, cease all dealings with respect to commercial or industrial enterprises or concessions in Namibia'. The fact that the Atomic

[2]Ibid., p.21.

Energy Authority of the British government has financed the Rio Tinto Zinc company in order to assist it to develop its concession for a massive uranium mine at Rossing (Namibia) by promising to purchase the uranium when produced seems to have been ignored by the British public as one of those flagrant violations of principle which occur for the sake of self-interest. It is no wonder when countries disregard so blatantly resolutions for which they have voted that the United Nations is brought into disrepute, and Africans to despair.

The Namibian people have on the whole welcomed the efforts of the UN to solve their problems, though they did not take kindly to the UN Commissioner discussing their future with Prime Minister Vorster not so long ago. The only thing Namibians want from Vorster is their freedom, he has nothing else to say to them. The way other countries can help is by removing all investments from their country until such time as they achieve their independence. Sam Nujoma, President of SWAPO, re-stated this publicly in 1973 during the debate over South African wages. A further statement came to the UN General Assembly Fourth Committee in October 1973 from Mishake Muyongo, Acting Vice-Chairman of SWAPO. He recalled the Security Council's resolution asking all States to ensure that State-controlled enterprises did no business with Namibia, and that support be withheld from any company within a State which continues to trade with Namibia, and stated that, concerning such activities, almost all the Western nations stand accused. He went on, 'The conclusion is that a continuing economic and military aid from, and trade with, the United Kingdom, France, the United States, Germany and others, as well as the refusal of those countries to prohibit investment in Namibia and South Africa by their nationals and companies under their jurisdiction, continue to enable the South African regime to maintain the illegal occupation of Namibia'.[3]

In South Africa itself many of the non-white organizations representing various racial groups in the country have called on foreign investors to withdraw. The South African Trades Union Congress (SACTU), the only multiracial trade union organization in the country, which is now of course banned as a consequence of its non-racial stance, has adopted a policy of no foreign investment. Fatima Meer of the Indian Congress of South Africa at an address in the Interchurch Centre in New York in January 1973 told of a meeting attended by 10,000 Indians calling on foreign investors to pull out from their operations in the country. Sonny Leon, leader of the Coloured People's Labour Party, has echoed this call. Black students of the South African Students Organization (SASO) made a policy statement in 1972 which saw foreign investments as giving stability to the South Africa exploitative regime and committing the regime's trading partners to its support. The only black people's political party operating in South Africa, the Black People's Convention (BPC) stated at their Conference in December 1972, 'Foreign investors in this country claim their presence

[3]Ibid., p.24

contributes towards the development of the black community. This claim is disputed by the reality of black experience in this country. We therefore resolve:

> To reject the involvement of foreign investors in this exploitative economic system;
>
> To call upon foreign investors to disengage themselves from this white-controlled exploitative system.'

The BPC followed this up in March 1973 by directly asking all foreign investors to withdraw their investment.

The two Liberation Movements of South Africa itself have made their position plain. In a statement responding to the campaign by the World Council of Churches against investment in South Africa, Potlako Leballo, the Acting President of the Pan Africanist Congress, stated that the World Council had given an exemplary lead to Christians and justice-loving people the world over. He went on: 'To the apologists who maintain that African people will also suffer as a result of withdrawal of investment from South Africa our answer is: our people will suffer no more than the Indochinese whose population has been massacred in millions, whose fields, forests and rivers have been crudely bombed and polluted. This is a sacrifice our people are prepared to make.' The African National Congress has spoken out equally strongly, and ANC spokesmen made several policy statements following the *Guardian* disclosures in March 1973. In a letter to the newspaper, Reg September, Chief Representative of the ANC in Europe, pointed out that the cheap labour system is fundamental to the socio-economic system of South Africa, and raising wages does not guarantee the end of exploitation. In the final analysis, September argued, the only solution is the complete dismantling of the socio-economic structure, and the return of the country to the people. Elsewhere the ANC has stated that liberal opinion which does not accept the need for withdrawal is only delaying the necessary basic change. Oliver Tambo, speaking as the Acting President of the ANC at Addis Ababa in May 1973 stated that Africans were prepared to suffer unemployment and sacrifice if companies would withdraw their interests. There might then develop a 'peaceful crisis' situation within the country.

International economic sanctions have been a vital plank in the ANC policy since Chief Lutuli spelled out the Africans' willingness to suffer for their freedom at the beginning of the last decade. Nelson Mandela, President of the ANC, speaking from the dock in the 1964 Treason Trials, before he was sentenced to life-imprisonment, gave some of the reasons why the ANC turned to sabotage: 'We believed that South Africa depended to a large extent on foreign capital and foreign trade. We felt that planned destruction of power plants, and interference with rail and telephone communications, would tend to scare away capital from the country . . . and would in the long run be a heavy drain on the economic life of the country, thus compelling the voters to re-think their position'.

The worm may be one of the lowliest creatures, but at the same time it may possess the best vantage point from which to discern real human quality and kindness. The worm's eye view often sees the truth writ largest of all. There is a profound Christian doctrine about the value of weakness, powerlessness, suffering and sacrifice. The Western churches at the present time could learn quite a bit about crucifixion from the African Liberation Movements.

Finally, an article in *The Times* in January 1975 reported one of the most representative gatherings ever of 320 South African blacks, including educationalists, professional groups, trade unionists, students, and both Protestant and Roman Catholic churchmen. All racial groups were represented, and the convention totally rejected the government's policy of separate 'Homelands'. It called for a united and democratic South Africa in which all citizens would participate (even a Homelands Minister was ejected from the meeting, despite his stand on behalf of South African political prisoners). Lastly the meeting demanded an international boycott of the racial South African government in cultural, educational, economic, labour and military relations. There could be no plainer statement than that.

5 Of elephants and jaguars

The churches' response

SO, IN THE MIDST of discussion, debate, racial injustice and guerrilla war, where have the churches stood? Too often the answer has been, with one major exception, as far away as possible. The picture of the churches in Western Europe has been one of elephantine medieval organizations, still living on the riches of the past, and fearful to compromise those riches in order to take a stand for the principles on which the organizations once were based. The American church has not been in existence so long, so that the creeping effects of institutional *rigor mortis* have not gained such a hold. Nevertheless the only real exception to this gloomy picture is the World Council of Churches. Why has this been the case? Perhaps because it stands so much in the crossfire of international debate, perhaps because it possessed the right leaders with their ears open to the right people, perhaps because God can still take hold even of an ecclesiastical machine and turn it into a prophetic instrument of the Gospel. It has the additional advantage of being under 33 years old, the age beyond which humanity often turns from crucifixion to compromise. However this exception is to be explained, among the oppressed of the world, and particularly among the people of Africa, the image of the Christian Church has taken on a new dimension because of the World Council's stand on international racism. Let us then trace briefly the development of the WCC's awareness before examining the response of some of its member churches.

The World Council of Churches

Involvement in the question of racial exploitation can be traced back to the World Council's consultation on Church and Society in 1966, and the Fourth Assembly, at Uppsala (Sweden) in 1968. At Uppsala, for the first time a substantial number of young people were invited to join the international church leaders in their deliberations, and speakers like Kenneth Kaunda and James Baldwin, the black US novelist, were invited from beyond the confines of the traditional Church. This led to a worldly breath of realism blowing through the Assembly and eventually to the setting up of the Programme to Combat Racism (PCR) by the WCC Central Committee in 1969. The story of the whole Programme is told in Elisabeth Adler's book *A Small Beginning,* but here we are concerned chiefly with the specific involvement of the Programme in the issue of investment in southern Africa, and the way in which this investment has helped to maintain both the exploitation of black workers and the income of the Western church.

The basis on which the PCR was drawn up was that of a redistribution of power, and this was to be achieved in several ways. One was the Special Fund to Combat Racism, raising money specifically for groups struggling against racial injustice, to which the World Council committed $200,000 of its own reserves as a gesture of sacrifice. The reaction of British Church leaders was predictable. A former Secretary of the British Council of Churches, the Rev. Kenneth Slack, was quoted in the *Methodist Recorder* as questioning the correctness of such unwise action. Presumably the dictates of the Gospel were never meant to be actually put into practice, merely read out in Church for the benefit of a well-fed, insured and comfortable people. Needless to say the British contributions to the Fund have been pathetic. The only official donation has been £4,000, given over four years by the Methodist Missionary Society, and up to the end of 1974 British giving had been a derisory 1½ per cent. of the total Fund of over a million dollars.

But as we have said, our chief concern here is with investment, though the figures for donations give some indication of what the response was likely to be to other parts of the PCR. Investment was in fact the second major area in which the PCR felt action could be taken to redistribute power in southern Africa. The subject first appeared on the Programme's agenda in 1972, and at the Central Committee meeting in Utrecht (Holland) in August of that year a resolution was put to the effect that, considering the effect of foreign investment in southern Africa was to strengthen the white minority regimes, the Finance Committee should sell any existing holdings, and make no further investments, in companies which invest in, or trade with, any of the countries of that region. Furthermore it should deposit none of its funds in banks which maintain direct banking operations in southern Africa. Secondly the WCC urged all member churches, Christian agencies, and individual Christians to use all their influence, including share-holder action and disinvestment, to press corporations to withdraw investment from, and to cease trading with, the whole area.

It may be useful at this point just to distinguish between the use of the terms 'withdrawal' and 'disinvestment'. 'Withdrawal' is used of the action, or proposed action, of a company in pulling out its investment, selling its interests, or closing down its plant. 'Disinvestment' however refers to the action of shareholders, or investors, with regard to the stock they hold. It may include the technique of selling the vast majority of a shareholding, but retaining a small interest in order to continue pressure on the company.

It was acknowledged by the WCC that not all its member churches could support its stand, though the vote at Utrecht was almost unanimous, and none of the British representatives voted against.

There was a suggestion from the Evangelical Church in Germany that 'multiple strategies' should be worked out, and that pressure for change through reform should be attempted initially. In the pamphlet *Time to*

Withdraw the PCR outlined the possible alternative strategies, 'Increased involvement', 'Reform', and 'Withdrawal'. Let us then examine in outline these three strategies for change.

(a) Increased Involvement. This was suggested by those who felt that more investment would give investors increased power to change things, but this can be shown up as a pipedream in two ways. Firstly, increased investment presumably refers partly to the kind of investment which would directly benefit black people, and for which some Africans like Chief Buthelezi have actually called. However as long ago as 1954 the Tomlinson Commission reported to the South African government, which had set it up to explore the amount of money needed to develop the Bantu 'Homelands', that $1\frac{1}{4}$ million jobs should be created in the Bantustans. To date only 1,000 jobs have been created there, with another 50,000 in the 'border areas', where investors are wooed with the promise of government grants, and waived minimum pay levels. Tomlinson estimated that the Bantustans, even with only 13 per cent. of the country's land, could support two million people, and that if 50,000 new jobs per year were found for 30 years, most of the African population could eventually be supported there. Not only was this based on a considerable underestimate of population growth, but the cynical disregard by the government of the amount of land and money needed has rendered the whole plan useless.[3]

Secondly, South Africa already depends enormously on its inflow of capital. Overseas investors could have changed things radically years ago, if they had really wished to do so. But as we have seen they have not, nor do they show much sign of being prepared even to countenance the major shifts required within South African society. Increased involvement in South Africa's economy only strengthens apartheid and there is no evidence whatever to show that Britain's increasing involvement over the last 70 years has improved the lot of the Africans at all.

(b) Reform. This strategy is generally understood to mean the improvement of wages, working conditions, pensions, etc. for African, Coloured and Asian workers. Such changes are to be brought about by putting pressure on foreign companies in their home countries by delegations, boycotts, shareholder questioning, protest campaigns, etc. It is then expected that the companies will make some inprovements for their black workers, but neither the taxing need for an almost permanent campaign, nor the indignity of the African worker who has had to rely on others to get his rightful wage for him, seems to be taken into account by those who advocate this kind of action. The 'Polaroid experiment' has been the one looked to to provide a test-case for the reform argument. In January 1971, after a demand from black American workers to withdraw from South Africa, Polaroid announced that its South African subsidiary would increase wages, offer educational grants to its workers, and cease to deal directly with the South

[3]Cosmas Desmond, *The Discarded People*, pp.30-1.

African government. At the end of a year the South African *Financial Mail* reported that workers were still being paid the local minimum, that is, below subsistance level; Africans who were given opportunities of education still had to take them within the apartheid system, and Polaroid advertisements were still stating in October 1971 that the South African government were the largest users of their ID3 Identification System (see *Time to Withdraw,* WCC Report, pp.11-12).

Tim Smith, now working for the Interfaith Centre for Corporate Responsibility of the U.S. National Council of Churches, has visited South Africa and studied industrial conditions there. He continues to work on the responsibilities of American corporations in southern Africa. He does not believe that the policy of reform has altered the basic power relationship in South African society at all, and regards the integration of a few African workers at the lower skilled levels of industry as only the very beginning of change. The distribution of power remains the same, held firmly in the hands of the whites, management and workers combined; the only results are a nation of slightly better fed and clothed political and economic serfs. He goes on, 'By pressing for certain limited economic reforms, but not for deep-rooted change, liberal industrialists will be able to achieve a number of economic objectives:

greater productivity than is possible with white workers;

a regular supply of cheap labour;

production at lower cost, due to low wages paid to blacks for doing the same job as whites;

maintenance of the white community's high standard of living;

ability to compete in the export market, especially in the rest of Africa, and so increase their political stranglehold on the continent."[2]

Time to Withdraw comments that in considering the 'Reform' argument it must be noted that the denial of trade union rights to African workers has always been a key to apartheid both in practice and in principle. If this argument takes itself seriously this must be the most fundamental area in which shareholders are to generate pressure.

(c) Withdrawal. The final possible strategy for shareholders in companies with southern African interests is 'Withdrawal', by one means or another requesting the company to cease its operations in that region. One of the chief reasons firms invest there is cheap labour, and one of the chief reasons for cheap labour is the totally inadequate proportion of African-owned land. Therefore millions of Africans have no alternative but to take whatever wages are offered to them in the factories and mines of foreign companies. But these companies have never done anything at all about the shortage of African land; they prefer Africans to have no choice where to work, since it puts the companies in such a strong position. This whole labour system contributes to the very high living standard of the white

[2]Timothy Smith, *American Corporations in South Africa.*

community, and to the upkeep of the forces they need to defend themselves. The fact that much of South Africa's military equipment could be used internally as much as externally speaks for itself.

Western companies are quite happy to see this state of affairs develop. For one thing, many of the arms purchases are made from them, despite UN resolutions requesting no sale of arms to South Africa. For another thing, it means their interests will be well-protected if any trouble starts. This has already been made plain. Riots at mines or factories involving Africans are put down with the use of force, if necessary by shooting to kill. The total of nearly 50 miners killed in the eight months from September 1973 to April 1974 testifies to this. There is no understanding that the Africans have no other channel through which to air their grievances, or if they have that it is totally controlled by the establishment. And here we touch on one of the most unpleasant aspects of the whole situation, that if the Africans are ever able, despite the enormous odds, to organize sufficiently to threaten the apartheid system, the call to Britain will be very much that we must go in and support our 'kith and kin'. South African whites would have to be protected from black 'savagery', not forgetting all the money we have poured into mining equipment and industrial plant over the last 50 years. The builder Neil Wates, even when given a free and spectacular guided tour of the country by its backers, was quite adamant that it was impossible to invest in South Africa without getting caught up in the system by which it is run. Many of the British companies which gave evidence to the Commons sub-committee tacitly agreed. There is no escape from the vicious and entwining web of apartheid, except by withdrawing from the whole situation.

Thus having gone through the arguments for the three strategies the WCC decided by an overwhelming majority to accept the resolutions calling for the selling of its own shares, and for shareholder action by its member churches. Lists of corporations with interests in southern Africa were published, and the Churches of the West were challenged to take up the resolutions for which the World Church had voted, and to act upon them. The World Council jaguar was showing its teeth.

The American scene

Before examining the activity — or perhaps we should say 'inactivity' — of the British churches, let us take a look at the scene on the other side of the Atlantic, partly because it gives us a number of models as to how the churches here might have gone about things, and the kind of tactics that can usefully be employed. The North American churches have been concerned about this whole matter for some ten years now. One of their first major campaigns, begun in 1966, concerned loans of $40m by ten United States banks to the South African government. This included two of the largest banks in the world, and the campaign involved letters of protest, delegations to the banks, questions at shareholders' meetings, withdrawal of funds, picketing, leaflets and demonstrations. The most significant single action was the decision of the United Methodist Board of Missions to remove a $10m. investment portfolio from First National City Bank. Altogether some $23m of objectors' money was removed from the banks. Congressmen protested to the bankers, as did black leaders, and the UN General Assembly voted to terminate its own transactions with these banks. In November 1969 the loans were closed, very largely as a result of the protest campaign.

Since then the statements and actions of U.S. Churches have grown stronger and more direct. In 1971 John Hines, Presiding Bishop of the Episcopal Church, not renowed as one of the most revolutionary elements in U.S. society, put out a statement to clergy on 'Social Responsibility with Church Investments'. He pointed out the need for churches to exercise responsible stewardship over the funds entrusted to their care and invited the clergy to support the Executive Council's shareholder resolutions on U.S. business involvement in Puerto Rico, and in South Africa. The purpose of the latter resolutions was to question the support given by companies to the exploitative system of apartheid. Such resolutions, he admitted, would be unlikely to succeed, but they would raise the level of debate both in the companies and in society itself about the implications of being involved in southern Africa. The statement concluded with suggestions for action, mainly supporting church resolutions at four company meetings, including Gulf Oil, General Motors and American Metal Climax.

The fact that this kind of public action was being undertaken so long ago in the United States is quite astonishing in the context of the widespread apathy, evasion and downright opposition prevalent among British churches. The Episcopal Church was not of course the only one to make this kind of commitment. The U.S. United Methodist Board of Missions, meeting in April 1972, reaffirmed a strong statement made in 1968, to the effect that:

> 'We are concerned with the continued basic denial of human rights in South Africa, Zimbabwe, Angola, Mozambique and Namibia;
> We are convinced that the struggle for freedom by the majority population in south Africa will be won;
> We see as Christians a strategic mission issue, in terms of assisting forces that are likely to bring changes leading to justice and peace;
> We urge that our Church be mobilised with all its energies, that our government and industry be sensitised to our inescapable obligations in southern Africa.'

The statement goes on to discourage the U.S. Methodist Church from investing in those U.S. companies which have interests in southern Africa, and if it is ascertained that they support white minority rule, the church should press them to cease doing business there. Then, as a minimum requirement:

> We urge that any income from Church investment in corporations which invest in southern Africa, or an equivalent amount, be given to an enlarged Board of Missions 'Southern Africa Fund';
>
> We urge that the Church seek from all corporations doing business in southern Africa the facts of their involvement, including the history, and relations with workers and government, and ask these facts be made public;
>
> We recommend that the Church urge all U.S. Corporations doing business in southern Africa to contribute a sum equal to a substantial proportion of the amount which they are required to pay yearly to the governments of the area in taxes:
>
> > to the educational, medical and welfare programmes of the Liberation Movements;
> >
> > to those organisations supportive of racial justice and basic social change;
> >
> > to the UN Trust Fund for southern Africa for the victims of racialism or colonialism.'

A series of standards were then laid down for all the investments of the Mission Board of the United Methodist Church, including the refusal of donations which demanded continuing investment in ethically unsatisfactory companies. These principles were then taken up by the Board's various Divisions. For example a Report on the actions of the Women's Division in early 1972 includes such items as:

'(1) South Africa banking consortium, visited bank officials, sold First, National City Bank bonds;

(2) Vietnam War, sold Dow Chemical stock to protest against the manufacture and sale of napalm;

(6) Campaign General Motors, voted the Divisions shares as a proxy with groups challenging G.M.'s activities in South Africa and elsewhere.'

A campaign of shareholder action on all kinds of issues was thus well under way in this Division in 1972, including the selling of shares if the company refused to listen to what the church had to say. The discussion was taken to top level in the U.S. Methodist Church by a Report adopted by the Council on Finance and Administration in November 1973, and southern Africa was stated as one of the areas for concern and action.

In 1971 there was published in the United States a document entitled *Corporate Responsibility and Religious Institutions.* It was produced by the staff of the Corporate Information Center (CIC) which had then just been set up by the U.S. National Council of Churches, and other religious groups.

The document stated the aims of the CIC to be research into the activities of corporations for the churches, and to suggest possible varieties of action which could be taken. The document included an article on 'The Investment Responsibilities of Boards Concerned about Human Welfare' by the Chairman of the Episcopal Investment Committee; 'Why are the Churches getting involved in investments?' by the Treasurer of the U.S. Baptist Home Mission Society; and 'An Investment Adviser's View-point' by an Account Executive with a firm of investment brokers. Hence the churches were generating a public debate about social responsibility in investments at a very high level, not just among clergy, but also among laity who had key posts in the world of finance. Since then the activities of the CIC have expanded considerably, and it has become the Interfaith Center for Corporate Responsibility (ICCR) employing six full-time staff members.

The ICCR has been a crucial force in the development of the U.S. church-shareholder action campaign. It is financed by ten church bodies, including the American Baptist Church, the Friars of the Atonement, the United Church of Christ (Congregational), the United Methodists, the United Presbyterians and the Episcopalians. It appears to have come about because of the dedicated hard work of its Director, Frank White, and his chief assistant Tim Smith, though the far-sightedness of the church bodies prepared to put up the money must also be commended. ICCR's plans for shareholder action include delegations to management, proposing critical resolutions at company meetings (or supporting the resolutions of others), voting to change the management, soliciting proxy votes from other shareholders, bringing law-suits, disinvesting, and publicizing the reasons for all of these. There is thus a variety of actions which might be undertaken by the church investor, either alone, or in concert with other concerned bodies, churches, universities, or charitable foundations.

The activities of the ICCR have caused much press interest in the United States. A *New York Times* article in January 1974, entitled 'Church Group Hits Corporations' covers the planned activities of the ICCR through 1974, including resolutions that asked U.S. companies to withdraw from Mozambique, Angola and Guiné, and to refuse investment in South African 'border areas', which only enable the government to get the workers out of the city, pay them lower wages, and cement the apartheid system. The *Wall Street Journal* has published a number of articles on church stockholder campaigns. It is arguable that publicity is in fact the churches' most effective weapon. So far the churches in Britain have not even begun to use it.

In October 1973 the ICCR brought out another detailed report on 'Church Investments, Corporations and Southern Africa'. It gave a background to apartheid, dealt in detail with the 15 largest corporations in southern Africa, and gave information on a total of 53 companies altogether. It also listed the church investments in these 53, and gave examples of the sort of action churches might take. One of the largest U.S. investors in

South Africa, and the largest corporation in the world, is General Motors (GM). The ICCR Report quotes from GM's own statement on 'Progress in Areas of Public Concern', which gives detailed information on wages and benefits of all workers. It is of typical of such statements, showing that nearly all the African workers are in grades 1-4, a number of Coloureds are to be found up to grade 7, and the vast majority of white workers are in grades 8-11. At the time of this Report, over 90 per cent. of GM's African workers, and 80 per cent. of its Coloured workers, were paid below the MEL.

This disclosure of information came about largely because of the persistence of groups like ICCR. The debate on withdrawal from South Africa has been forced open, even though as yet the Company is resisting by all the arguments it can muster a serious consideration of whether it ought to pull out. The wages and conditions of black South African workers in British firms and their subsidiaries have been made public to some extent by the House of Commons sub-committee. So far however the churches here have failed to take advantage of the facts available to put pressure on companies in the way the Americans have done.

The 'Programme of Corporate Challenges for 1974', produced by the ICCR, outlined ninety resolutions to be presented to companies in eight areas of social concern. By far the largest of these areas was southern Africa, and this section included resolutions to twenty-two different companies, by nine church bodies. Some of these involved what were still then the Portuguese colonies, others dealt with Namibia, border industries in South Africa, 'Review Committees' to be set up by companies operating in southern Africa, and 'disclosure resolutions' asking companies to reveal full information about the way they operate in Zimbabwe or South Africa.

An example of the kind of debate generated by these resolutions is shown by what happened to one directed at the Newmont Mining Company which controls the largest Tsumeb mine in Namibia. Equal Employment Opportunity, or EEO, is an important facet of the race relations laws in the United States. It requires all companies to employ a fair proportion of people from all races, to pay them equal wage rates, and to give them equal opportunity of training, promotion, etc. The theme of a number of church resolutions has been that companies should be required to follow the same employment practices abroad as they do at home. The Newmont Company was chosen as a particularly bad example of a company which exploited its workers in extreme fashion when it thought it could get away with it. The actual resolution, by two Boards of the United Church of Christ, pointed out that average white wages were six times average black ones, which meant that some Africans were earning very poor wages indeed. The company put up a strong fight, and refused even to discuss the terms of the resolution with UCC. The church sponsors of ICCR reckon on the whole they have failed if they need to bring resolutions to the floor of a company meeting now. They hope for most of their requests to be conceded beforehand, though companies often only accede to ICCR's requests because they know they will be caused a fair degree of embarrassment if they refuse. In the final analysis the UCC was forced to take almost a full-page advertisement on the *Wall Street Journal* in order to explain to shareholders exactly what Newmont was doing. To their surprise they reached the 3 per cent. of the vote at the AGM which enables the resolution to be repeated next year, and is therefore the first step to victory. This was largely because for the first time one of the insurance companies, which usually remain studiously neutral in such matters, voted for the UCC resolution.

It was another UCC resolution, on prospecting in Namibia, which brought what Dr Howard Schomer, executive of the UCC Board of World Ministries, called 'the first withdrawal victory in the stockholder campaign'. Four large oil companies had been involved in a consortium prospecting for oil off the coast of Namibia; Getty, Phillips, Standard Oil of California and Continental Oil (Conoco). Different sponsors of ICCR had shares in each of these companies, and four Departments of the United Church, including the Pension Fund, had shares in Conoco amounting to a total of $8m. The resolution stated that the companies should cease their explorations immediately, as they had only been granted concessions by the South African government, not by the people of Namibia. It was also official policy of the U.S. government not to invest in Namibia until the country was under the control of its own people. In September 1974 Conoco announced that it had withdrawn from the consortium and would take no further part in any investment in Namibia until there was a freely-elected government. This was not therefore an actual withdrawal of an existing operational enterprise, but it was a significant victory for the ICCR campaign.

The activities in the United States have not gone unnoticed in Australia and Canada. The Australian Council of Churches in August 1974 sent a letter signed by prominent Australian Christians to all companies investing in southern Africa, requesting full information on their operations there. The Canadian Anglican Church and the United Church of Canada have both joined ICCR in discussion and action involving Canadian companies with U.S. subsidiaries, and *vice versa*. Companies confronted include Alcan and Falconbridge, both large mining operations, Gulf Oil, then paying large taxes to keep the Portuguese Army fighting to protect its Angolan oil, and General Foods, busy importing coffee from the exploited plantations of Angola. The United Church of Canada set up in 1973 a Committee on Investing Church Funds for Social Purposes which produced a Report 'All That Money Can Buy'. This discussed not only what the Church should not invest in, including southern Africa, but also what it could invest in positively, to use its money constructively, for example low-cost housing. The Canadian churches are also involved in the 'Banks Campaign' begun in the United States when it was discovered that American and European banks were involved in a series of direct loans to the South African government.

Loans to South Africa

The 'Banks Campaign' has been one point at which the whole investment issue had had a real chance of developing an international dimension, and its progress to the beginning of 1975 provided a comparison of activity on opposite sides of the Atlantic. The loans involved banks in the U.S.A., Canada, and several European countries, and the campaign began in 1973 when a member of ICCR received secret information from someone high up in one of the banks involved. That information turned out to be dynamite, in that it was revealed that a total of eleven American, three Canadian and six European banks had combined together through the multinational Banking group EABC (European-American Banking Corporation) to lend $210m (£90m) to agencies of the South African government, including the Ministry of Finance itself. The EABC is owned by banks from Germany, France, Austria, Holland, Belgium and Britain, our representative being the Midland. The loans began in 1970, at a crucial time for the faltering South African economy. At that point there seems to have been a real possibility that the 'economic argument' might have worked, that economic forces beyond South Africa's control might have conspired to bring the system down. But when there really seemed some likelihood of that happening foreign interests, far from shouting 'Hurray! We've done it at last', as some would have us believe they intend, rushed in with bank loans to shore up a tottering economy. In early 1975 the loans were still continuing, and more had been arranged, especially with ISCOR, the South African Iron and Steel Corporation.

Whatever the argument about foreign investment, and the difficulty of withdrawing it, there is no real problem about bank loans. They could be called in at a few months' notice. Also they do not even help British trade, which the 'reformers' think might be a good thing. They directly support the government, responsible for the misery and inhumanity of apartheid, and they lend in Euro-dollars not sterling. This was thus a tailor-made opportunity for the European churches to join their American and Canadian counterparts in an international campaign to persuade the banks to withdraw. The Americans, by dint of hard campaigning and involvement of all kinds of groups, local authorities, charities, black community groups, had succeeded by the end of 1974 in persuading two banks to withdraw completely from the loans and four others to declare they would become involved no further. Five Canadian church bodies were enquiring as to the Canadian banks' position on the matter, and were planning action if there was a negative reply. The World Council of Churches had also taken an interest, and the banks issue had become part of the Programme to Combat Racism, and its general attack on investment in southern Africa.

The WCC had in fact stated in 1972 its determination to withdraw funds from all banks involved in southern Africa. During 1974 the Central Committee asked member churches to call on their national banks to withdraw any loans. In the six European countries whose banks own the EABC there was however a less than enthusiastic response. The Dutch churches made some effort to tackle the Amsterdam-Rotterdam Bank (Amro). The German churches had decided not to approach the Deutsche Bank. In Britain a group called ELTSA (End Loans to Southern Africa) was campaigning against the Midland Bank, but apart from a donation by the Methodist Church, and a couple of questions at the 1974 Midland AGM by Methodist shareholders little response had come from the British churches. That was the sum of church action on this issue in Europe 18 months after the original revelations.

One or two points made by the Midland Bank in response to ELTSA's campaign may illuminate the wholly negative way in which the world of finance and commerce views this whole matter. The Chairman of the Bank, in a statement at the AGM in 1974, said that banks only respond to business criteria, not those of politics or, by implication, those of morality. This of course is quite untrue. International banks consistently refused to assist President Allende of Chile when he needed to raise loans, largely because they did not like his politics. Statements by the bank have also referred protesters to the government, saying that it is their responsibility to make such decisions about the customers to whom this country should lend. This again implies that commerce can only be expected to be amoral, something which many leading figures in business would resent, including Mr Neil Wates. Another typical ploy is to draw on sympathy for the blacks in South Africa by stating that they will be the ones to suffer most. This of course is only said by those who have little idea what black South Africans are saying, except what the conservative British press reports, and it is also a position which we refute in our last chapter. One thing the Midland Bank had said which is justified is that South Africa is a substantial trading partner which Britain would find it difficult to do without. This is quite true, but nobody said that apartheid was going to be brought down without sacrifice, least of all the Africans, and a little good business may be one of the sacrifices we have to make.

The British Churches

The example of Midland Bank gives an illustration of the kind of pressure the British churches could wield if they chose to work together, and the sort of shareholdings they have in many companies involved in apartheid. The list of Midland shareholders includes the Church Army, with 5,000 shares, the Church of England Children's Society (9,000), the Church of Ireland Trustees (5,000), the Church of Scotland (9,300), the old Congregational Union (5,500), the Baptist Union of Scotland (5,000), the Methodist

Missionary Society (5,000), the Methodist Central Finance Board (20,000) and, as usual the largest, the Commissioners of the Church of England (590,000). These were the figures in early 1974; other shareholders include a substantial number of clergymen, and various charitable organisations likely to be run by church people. Local authorities are another group of major shareholders. Out of the 150 shareholders the ELTSA group wrote to in late 1974 only four church bodies replied. The Scottish Baptists, the Church Commissioners, and the Methodist Missionary Society and Finance Board said they had taken the matter up with Midland, but none of them would state publicly what Midland had said, or whether they were prepared to take the matter further. Nor did they seem inclined to come together to plan some kind of concerted action. It was in response to such a request for co-ordination that a spokesman for the Church Commissioners, by far the most powerful ecclesiastical investors, stated that the Commissioners considered it was far better for them to express their concerns to management individually, rather than become involved with other church bodies in an ecumenical approach. One can only hazard a guess at why they do not wish to associate their protest with those of other, poorer, but often equally conservative Christian bodies.

It might be opportune at this point to comment on the power held by the Church of England in these matters, and particularly the Church Commissioners. A number of church financiers in Britain have been heard to say that it is all right for the Americans to mount these shareholder campaigns for improved wages, withdrawal of investment, or whatever, but the American churches are much wealthier than the British. This may to some extent be true, though the chief weapon of the churches remains publicity, and the discomfort with which the average company would view a public confrontation with church bodies on ethical questions. The Church Commissioners are however one of the largest financial institutions in the country; their assets were conservatively estimated at £600m in 1973,[3] of which well over half was invested on the stock exchange. That is a lot of money, and it is a lot of power. When challenged about their use of this power the Commissioners point out that they do not invest in certain socially unacceptable practices, such as armaments, tobacco and alcohol, or since 1972 in firms whose major operations are in South Africa. Nevertheless, in 1973, the Commissioners' investments included £1.5m in British Leyland, over £4m in GEC, £1m in Metal Box, £1¼m in Barclays Bank and around £4m in ICI, all companies with considerable interests in southern Africa, although this is not the area of their 'major operations'. Other church bodies of course have substantial interests in these companies also.

The Commissioners claim that they make their views known to any company in which they have shares, and with whose policy they disagree.

---

[3] *Business Observer,* 28 October, 1973.

Unfortunately they refuse not only to divulge their portfolio, the list of their investments, but also which companies they have approached, and the nature of the response. Nor have they any stated policy about what action they might take if a particular company was deemed to have overstepped the grounds of ecclesiastical decency. The only clue as to what might happen came in September 1972 when at the British Council of Churches 'Church Leaders Conference' the Commissioners were accused of involvement in modern-day slavery through their investments in Rio Tinto Zinc. The Commissioners responded almost immediately by saying they had already sold their shares, though they never stated exactly why they had picked on RTZ, merely referring to a general statement that they did not invest in firms operating wholly or partly in southern Africa. RTZ in fact does not operate anything like wholly in southern Africa, but the Commissioners were not prepared to particularize their statement.

There are two points to note about this situation. Firstly no one would have known the Commissioners owned £1.5m of RTZ stock had not research by volunteers revealed the information. Secondly nobody would have known the shares had been sold, or why, if there had not been a BCC meeting at which the Commissioners could be publicly confronted and before which they almost had to answer. The Church Commissioners are in fact stewards of public funds, money given long ago by the nation for the support of the Church. They therefore have no moral right to refuse any church member, or indeed any British citizen, full information as to what their investments are, and what they are doing with them. Their policy however is a private, secret and negative one, in that they appear to believe that, if there *is* anything wrong with a company in which they hold shares, a few words on the old-boy network will ensure all is well. Incidentally it was reported that the Methodist Annuitant Society also sold their shares in RTZ during 1974, but not many Methodists seem to have been informed of this prophetic action.

There is thus no real feeling of commitment in the world of church finance to the demands of the Christian Gospel, which does happen to include a prophetic element in which the mighty are brought down from their seats, the poor are exalted and the rich sent empty away. The plea that the clergy must have pay and pensions is not sufficient. Should the clergy really be paid at the expense of oppression, injustice and poverty in southern Africa? Should churches truly be kept open by the sweat of miners who will not see their families for another 11 months? There are many who feel redundant churches and their clergy at present hamper Christian mission in this country, and that a little less income and a little more planning and sharing might do the churches a world of good.

Discussion on investment has been going on in the Anglican Church since late 1973. In that time various resolutions have been passed, and two documents on investment in South Africa have been produced by the Anglican Board of Social Responsibility. These delineate clearly the rather shallow basis on which the Church of England is acting. No attempt is made to ask the fundamental question of how power may be redistributed in South Africa, nor is there any effort to think through theologically the prophetic stance being taken by the World Council of Churches. There is deep concern expressed about the possibility of violence, there is indignation about apartheid, there are various suggestions of how to deal with its more unpleasant manifestations, there is even a call for more African trade unions. At the same time, the philosophy behind the Reports is summed up in the quotation 'In South Africa, fortunately, long-term self-interest and moral obligation go hand-in-hand'[4]. That may be correct, but it has also been the self-justifying stance of a Christianity which has been involved in dialogue with wealth and power since Constantine. It no more represents a true Christian stance alongside the powerless now than it did then.

Further evidence of the superficiality of this approach can be seen in the Report's section on trades unions. The South African Congress of Trade Unions (SACTU) is not even mentioned, despite its long history of organising African labour. It is suggested that the white TUC of South Africa (TUCSA) be supported 'in its current attempt to make a stand for South African trade union rights'. As the members of TUCSA are one of the main reasons why South Africa's policy of apartheid survives there will be little confidence among Africans that change can come from this direction.

In the second Social Responsibility document, subtitled 'Opportunities for the Church', one of the suggestions is for assistance and investment directed to the African 'Homelands'. This is in response to calls for help from a particular sector of the African leadership. The fact is that support for the 'Homelands', which have a very limited 'independence', recognizes *de facto* the South African apartheid system. The document admits as much when it states that 'As far as the South African government is concerned there is considerable scope for improving African conditions within the context of the Republic's declared policies'.[5] The vital question of how those policies are to be changed is not considered.

The final 'Opportunity for the Church' described in the Report is 'the creation of an instrument, common to all churches and other interested bodies, which would centralize research and information on the whole future of South Africa'.[6] The Board of Social Responsibility saw such an instrument, under the direction of the BCC, as meriting full consideration by all the churches. Later the Anglicans not only sabotaged the possibility of a BCC 'instrument', they even refused at the Autumn General Synod in 1974 to make any donation to the alternative body 'Christian Concern for

[4] *Investment in South Africa; Challenge for the Church,* Anglican Board for Social Responsibility, p.6.

[5] *Investment in South Africa: Opportunities for the Church,* Anglican Board for Social Responsibility, p.4.

[6] Ibid, p.6.

Southern Africa', set up by concerned individuals within the churches. By this decision the Anglican Church showed where its interests really lay, beyond the rhetoric of resolutions and reports, and that is pretty firmly in its pocket.

But of course the other churches are no better. The Church of England tends to be singled out because it is the most powerful. Very few church bodies will readily open their books for inspection, so that their investments and the income from them may freely be examined. On enquiry, for example, the Methodist Central Finance Board states that it does not publish a list, because it would quickly become out of date. However, the Board receives a full list every six months, and although there are some changes the bulk of the list remains the same during such a period. Even if it is discovered they have shares in a questionable company, they will merely 'make representations' about their reservations. Despite the *Guardian* revelations, the House of Commons sub-committee Report, and the example of the U.S. Churches' activities, there has been no rush by our ecclesiastical elephants to do battle with the South Africa hyena. A summary of what the British Churches have actually achieved makes depressing reading . . .

The Baptists have passed a resolution in the Baptist Union Council expressing their concern, and have written to several companies, but they will not specify the number, let alone the names. The Roman Catholic Commission on Justice and Peace wrote to 450 religious orders in Great Britain asking them to take up the question of their investments as an important area of study; only one replied. A similar letter went to the Bishops in early 1975 and a rather more positive response was hoped for. The United Reformed Church has taken no action on this matter at all, apart from discussions in committee. The Church of England General Synod has passed some complicated and high-sounding resolutions; the Board of Social Responsibility has sent copies of its documents to the Chairmen of 45 major companies and the Commons sub-committee; the Central Finance Board were asked to sell shares in one of the more outrageously profitable gold-mining companies Consolidated Goldfields, but did not do so; the Church Commissioners have made their views known to an unspecified number of companies, and the Anglican Church as a whole has refused to vote any money to assess the effectiveness of its 'action' (which is one way of saying you don't really believe in what you're doing). The Methodist Conference passed by an overwhelming majority in 1971 a resolution that the Church should attend company meetings to express its concern; up to early 1975 a number of companies had been written to, several approached personally, one company meeting had been attended, and one question asked. The officers of the churches' finance sections seem able to ignore even the very mild democratically-arrived-at decisions of church assemblies, and to please themselves as to when, how, and if they will act on such decisions.

If the churches have failed to act as individuals, have they been any better in the mass, so to speak, as represented by the British Council of

Churches? There was in fact considerable discussion generated by the BCC during 1974 as to whether the churches could and would finance an instrument, or unit, specificially to deal with the investment question. In April 1973 the BCC Council had received a Report 'Investment in Southern Africa' prepared by a working group for the BCC's Department of International Affairs and the Conference of British Missionary Societies, which suggested that shareholder pressure, and if no response disinvestment, was the right strategy to deal with such investments. In October 1973 it was resolved to ask member churches if they would be prepared to support a common ecumenical instrument for this purpose.

By April 1974 there had been no adequate response from the churches, and the matter was left on the table, despite pressure from the Methodists. Decisions were complicated by the formation of a group outside the BCC, 'Christian Concern for Southern Africa', which was also in need of finance from the churches to do what the proposed BCC Unit was also to do.

During the summer of 1974 the General Secretary of the BCC, the Rev. Harry Morton became ill, and the care of the Unit was left in the hands of the Secretary for International Affairs, the Rev. Hugh Wilcox. The BCC Department of International Affairs has never shown any interest in any public radical action by the Churches on this issue, and the final recommendation via the Administrative Committee and the Executive to the October 1974 BCC Assembly seems to have been Wilcox's suggestion, then taken up by the General Secretary who had just recovered from illness. There is however nothing to show that the recommendation would have been any different had Harry Morton not been unwell. This resulted in a resolution that as there was inadequate financial response (only £6,000 out of a total of £10,000) the proposed Ecumenical Unit on Investment be cancelled. Churches were invited to support CCSA instead, leading Methodists including Rev. Derek Farrow of the Finance Board and Rev. Dr Colin Morris of the Missionary Society had stated they would appoint a staff person within the Methodist Church, though in the event they decided to support CCSA. There was thus a failure of nerve at this point by the BCC. They knew an Appeal had been prepared for the Roman Catholic Church by the Justice and Peace Commission, and it was likely that the remaining £4,000 could have been raised without too much difficulty, despite the refusal of the Anglicans to contribute. Finally it seems to have been much easier to wash the ecumenical hands.

This story is told in some detail just to illuminate how the British Church failed to meet the challenge of the major social issue of this decade. It failed by a mixture of ill-health, timidity, and obstructiveness, and the well-tried elephantine ecclesiastical tactic of squirting water at everyone else while making sure that you yourself don't get wet. It may be noted in passing that the Churches' Unity Commission, a dead duck if ever there was one, achieved its Budget requirement of around £10,000 from the churches in no time at all. Our giving so often shows up where our priorities lie.

Christian Concern for Southern Africa thus emerged in late 1974 as an escape route for the British churches from the debacle of the 'Investment Unit'. At that point CCSA was a heterogeneous unstructured group of individuals controlled by a Quaker, Trevor Jepson, and a Roman Catholic, Tim Sheehy. Its aims were outlined as research, production of reports, and arranging of seminars for businessmen and church leaders involved in investment in southern Africa. CCSA could become an alibi for the churches. Far from being a British version of the American ICCR it appeared to be developing as a buffer organization for those who wished to avoid confrontation. After all it is far safer to have a few more reports about low wages, untrained Africans and even unregistered trade unions, than it is actually to campaign for justice in the way requested by those who are oppressed. Besides which it takes nothing short of gelignite to get an unwilling ecclesiastical elephant out of its pew and on to the road. Some further research may be helpful, but the general facts of the situation are beyond dispute, and the World Council of Churches has already assessed the situation and outlined the strategy for changing it by campaigning for the withdrawal of investment. Jaguars, in comparison to elephants, are noted for rapidity of assessment and urgency of action. The British churches however seem as far from such dynamism as black African workers are from the company boardrooms and religious treasuries of distant Britain.

6 The owls and the pussycats

A theological perspective

THE MOST lively and interesting theology has always come from the front line of society, whether that line has been intellectual or activist. The three most productive eras in theological thought have been the early Christian centuries, when basic Christian theology was going through the furnace of its actual formation, the Reformation period, when many of the misconceptions which had grown up since that early period were rudely shattered, and the last hundred years, when Western man has had to come to terms with his new scientific, sociological and psychological world-view. It is arguable that we are now entering another great age of theology, which might be described broadly as 'political theology', arising from the realization that we have 'one world'. This means that our Christian teaching about freedom, justice, love and peace has to be put into practice throughout the world. And it is significant that front-line theology is no longer coming from the Western part, but from the 'developing' continents of Asia, Africa and Latin America. The theological owls have found younger, stronger trees in which to build their nests.

This new kind of theology appears to have been born somewhere in the awakening consciousness of black people, who at the same time as they were seeking social and political freedom began to seek a God and a theology of freedom as well. Thus was 'Black Theology' born in North America, and the 'Theology of Liberation' in the South. Our main concern lies with the interpretation of Black Theology and the Theology of Liberation by the Africans of southern Africa, but first, from whence does Black Theology derive its current inspiration?

One of the first books of this kind to appear was *Black Power and Black Theology* written in 1969 by James Cone, professor at Union Theological Seminary in New York. Accepting that he draws on a considerable historical tradition of developing thought by blacks, Cone says in his Introduction that the contemporary expression of this, 'Black Power', can evoke either angry rejection or passionate acceptance, but that its advocates hail it as the only viable option for black people. 'Black Power means black people taking the dominant role in determining the black-white relationship in society' (p.1). And if that frightens us a little, we may be experiencing a flicker of the atmosphere black people have had to endure for centuries, and still do in many parts of the world. Black Theology is the attempt to relate Christianity to the Black Consciousness movement. It develops however as a relationship very critical of traditional Christianity. Cone finds the crucial aspect of the relationship in the meaning of 'freedom', and liberation. Freedom implies the ability to make one's vision of oneself become true. Until now only white people have had the luxury of the possibility of such fulfilment of their dreams. Now, says Cone, speaking of the Gospel's power for freedom and service, 'Black Power and Christianity have this in common; the liberation of man!' And that liberation is of course for black *and* white; it has done white people no good to be in a position of supremacy for so long.

From Latin America comes a different style of theology, but one which finally is as critical, as difficult to hear and as creative for the contemporary theological search. It finds its most complete form so far in *A Theology of Liberation* by Gustavo Gutierrez. This is the book which heralds more than any other the new time of 'political theology', and it could become the most influential theological work of this half-century. Gutierrez's thesis is that the concept at the point of contact between theology and the world, the crucial point of the effectiveness of any theology, the theological 'front-line' as we have called it, is the concept of 'Liberation', with all its breadth of meaning. In Western theology salvation and eschatology have been very individual matters, but in African, Asian and Latin American theology we see a much more corporate concept of what Christianity is about. Can I really be saved if my brother or sister next to me is not?

Gutierrez probes critically into the concept of 'development', which we in the West have grown so fond of, as applied to the 'poor nations' upon whom we wish to visit our charity and our guilt. He points out that 'development' is in fact a ruse by which the rich world keeps itself rich, and the poor world poor, while tossing a few crusts of assistance here and there. He believes that the most important aspect of our understanding of man today 'is the struggle to construct a society of justice and brotherhood where people can live with dignity and be the agents of their own destiny. It is our opinion that the term "Development" does not well express these profound aspirations. "Liberation" on the other hand seems to express them better' (Introduction, p.x). Translation of this statement into the South African situation would find 'development' as the 'reform' of wages and conditions of African workers, and 'liberation' as the winning of political and economic justice by the Africans in their own country.

When we turn to the kind of theology which is coming from black South Africans in the realm of black consciousness and liberation our text-book must be *Black Theology — the South African Voice,* co-edited by Mokgethi Motlhabi and Basil Moore. The publication process of this book is itself an education in South African theology. The original editor Sabelo Ntwasa, who was to have edited conference papers on Black Theology, was placed under house arrest while the material was at the printers, which meant that everything he had written was banned. Of the two co-editors who then took over, Motlhabi was Director of the University Christian Movement's Black Theology Project until that was banned; Basil Moore, a Methodist minister also connected with the UCM was personally banned under the 'Suppression of Communism' Act, and came to Britain to work with the Student Christian Movement here. As the book went to press two more of its contributors, Steve Biko and Nyameka Pityana were also banned under the 'Suppression of Communism' Act. Pityana was again detained without trial at the end of 1974. It is not an easy life, being a frontier theologian in South Africa.

In his introduction to the book Basil Moore points out that although the title is imported from the U.S.A. the content emphatically is not. He talks of the failures of black and white, the whites who failed to see below the surface to what was happening both to their society and themselves, the blacks who even when educated failed to assist their fellow-Africans to develop in order to enter into some kind of equal relationship with whites. Most of all blacks could not rely on the 'liberal whites' who fought *for* them, but not *with* them. 'I cannot wholeheartedly trust a man who is fighting for me, for I fear that sooner or later he will tire of the struggle' (p.5). He sees these factors as being the chief ones that have led to the failure of multiracialism and the emergence of Black Consciousness, and, among church people, 'Black Theology'.

The spread of Black Consciousness in South Africa had largely been a phenomenon of the early 1970s. The prime movers of the concept have been the all-black South African Students Organisation (SASO), set up alongside the white students' National Union of South African Students around 1970. It is noticeable that it is SASO above all other groups among black Africans who have been the target for vilification, searches, arrests, bannings and all the other so-called legal paraphernalia of the South African 'judicial' system. The SASO policy manifesto adopted in 1971 states SASO's belief that South Africa is a country where black and white will continue to live together, but because of the problems whites have created blacks will be discouraged until they can speak with whites on equal terms. SASO defines black consciousness as an attitude of mind, as rejecting all value systems that reduce the black man's basic dignity, and as the development of awareness among black people of the power they hold both economically and politically. It aims for the spread of this consciousness throughout the black community, which will then develop its own solidarity before becoming involved in discussion and negotiation with white people about the way in which South African society must change.

The term 'black' is regarded as applying to all non-white people including Coloureds and Asians. Manifestations of Black Consciousness have been apparent in the areas of journalism and literature, trade unions, arts, entertainments and sports, as well as theology. The 1972 edition of *Black Review* quotes several responses to the idea of Black Consciousness. Most are critical, some anxiously self-justifying, but that of Nadine Gordimer at a lecture in the University of Natal is quoted as seeing Black Consciousness as a necessary step on the road to liberation. She sees the rejection of whites by blacks as a sign of 'healing negritude', and the role of the white liberal as working to set white society free from the lies on which it is built.

In the *Black Theology* collection the chapter on 'Black Consciousness' is by Nyameko Pityana. He criticizes strongly the role of the church and the missionary in the subjugation of black people throughout the whole colonial world, but particularly in southern Africa. 'The coming of Christianity set in motion a process of social change involving rapid disintegration of the tribal set-up and the framework of social norms and values by which people used to order their lives and relationships. The measure of one's Christian conviction . . . was in preserving the outer signs and symbols of the European ways of life', in manners, dress, hymn-tunes, and so on. 'European missionaries attacked the primitive rites of our people, condemmed our beautiful and soulful African tribal dances, recoiling from their suggestion on sensuality' (p.59). And he goes on to describe the process of how the white settlers, with the assistance of the church, robbed the black man of his soul, and deeply humiliated him. It is Black Consciousness which has seen the truth of this, and has liberated the African by so doing.

In his essay on 'The Concept of the Church in Black Theology' Sabelo Ntwasa also refers to the responsibility of the white church for creating the present situation. 'True to the wishes of its founders, it (the Church) is essentially the most colonial institution in the country today. Although the membership is 70 per cent. black, the power and the decision-making are still safely in the hands of the white minority'. He goes on, 'Black people in our country have largely resigned themselves to the fate of having other people decide what is good for them. But the worst thing they have done to themselves is to reject the traditional forms of expression and exalt the white man'. This, says Ntwasa, is where the case for Black Theology begins. 'Black Theology calls to black Christians to start defining the Christ-event for themselves . . . Black Theology describes Christ as a fighting God, not a passive God who allows a lie to exist unchallenged. Black Theology . . . seeks to return God to the black man, and to the truth and reality of his situation' (p.12).

Let the final word on Black Theology as such be from Mokgethi Motlhabi, the book's co-editor. He affirms that black theology is not a new theology nor is it a proclamation of a new Gospel. It is a revaluation of the Gospel message and it is fashioned for a particular people, at a particular time. The word 'black' in the context of Black Theology means 'suffering', because that is the standpoint from which it is written. Motlhabi restates the experiences we have heard above, that the missionaries and the white church have been a colonizing influence on the African, and have denounced African religion and culture. The Church hierarchy has helped to set up the apparatus of apartheid, and now claims to have turned from its evil ways. It preaches however what it does not practise. Ultimately however, says Motlhabi, and this is what must make Western theologians shiver in their shoes, 'Black Theology is not a theology of theory, but a theology of action, and development. It is . . . an authentic and positive articulation of our reflection on God in the light of our black experience' (p.80). So, at last it's out! A theology of action! A theology which involves confrontation and struggle and arrest and imprisonment. It's happened to Christians before, of course, but largely in spite of theology rather than because of it. And it has usually happened at crisis points in theological history — Hus, Luther, Galileo, Bonhoeffer — men who were all engaged in front-line theology, a theology of action. Why can the church still not read the signs of history?

The only essay which bravely attempts to spell out the practical consequences of Black Theology is by Steve Biko, perhaps not surprisingly the only writer besides Pityana who had no formal theological training. Even black theological training does its best to quench any spark of originality in a man, as Ntwasa describes in the book's penultimate chapter. Biko's political qualification is that he was the first President of SASO, and as was mentioned earlier, his determination to put thought into practice has led finally to his being banned. He examines the way racism has developed in South Africa, and notes the way white people even want to control the black reaction to their slavery. The thesis of the situation is a strong white racism. The antithesis is therefore not multiracialism, or integration, it is a strong black solidarity. The truth is expressed in the SASO cry, 'Black man, you are on your own!' It is the responsibility of Black Theology to relate the Christian Gospel to the black man's needs in his current situation. It is the duty of all black clergy to save Christianity for Africans by adopting the insights and the standpoint of Black Theology.

Steve Biko believes that Black Theology can restore to the black man the importance of humanity, the high regard for people and their property which has disappeared in the greed of the white man's system. The basis of racism is economic he argues, 'The leaders of the white community had to create some kind of barrier between blacks and whites so that the whites could enjoy privileges at the expense of the blacks, and still feel free to give a moral justification for the obvious exploitation that pricked even the hardest of white consciences' p.36. White churchmen today, even in Britain, still seek exactly the same kind of 'moral justification' for profiting from apartheid. 'Whites can help the blacks, by our investment and our expertise, and after all they do still need our help', such is our story, and our refrain. The blacks in South Africa today are objects of exploitation, states Biko, their cheap labour makes money for the whites, and their own money takes a one-way trip to white shops and banks. 'All we do in our lives is to pay the white man, either in labour or in coin.' Capitalism and racism have conspired against the African, 'Thus in South Africa now it is very expensive to be poor. It is the poor people who stay furthest from the town and therefore have to pay more money on transport to come and work for white people; it is the poor people who use uneconomic and inconvenient fuel because (there is) no electricity; it is the poor people who are governed by restrictive laws and have to pay fines for 'technical offences'; it is the poor people who use untarred roads, have to walk long distances, who experience the greatest wear and tear on their shoes; it is the poor who have to pay for the children's books while whites get them free. It does not need to be said that it is the black people who are poor' (p.46). Blacks, argues Biko, need to look more closely at how to use their economic power, little as it may be. Black co-operatives and banks, organization of black workers, boycotts of white business, these are the weapons which may bring justice. But that is the kind of talk which puts you in jail in South Africa. You may discuss the ideals of the Christian Gospel, of Black Consciousness, even of Black Theology. But mention economic sanctions, as the application of these ideals, and you are in real trouble. This is where the white community may be touched on its rawest nerve. And it is precisely here that the European churches have drawn back, like pussy-cats at the first sign of danger. Why? Perhaps just the usual human failings of selfishness, greed and fear.

Has the Western Church said anything theological in the one or two faltering steps it has taken towards political and economic action? Most of our theological wisdom today comes from the owls of the deep south, but perhaps a thought or two may still enter the mind of a pussy-cat. There are two sources available, on our particular subject, one from the British Council of Churches, the other from the WCC. Interestingly enough the former was not adopted by the BCC because the Department of International Affairs 'did not feel that its present form it should be submitted'. That can mean only two things, either the Report was so bad it should never have been written, or it was much too radical for the BCC. It is entitled 'Violence and Southern Africa' and one of the chapters concerns 'Revolution, the Church and the Kingdom of God'. It talks of an emerging 'theology of revolution', that is 'a readiness in many parts of the Church to consider the relation between man's continuing struggle for justice on earth, and the teaching of Jesus about the Kingdom of God' (p.69). The Report later takes up the issue of an economic boycott of South Africa because, it says, all possible methods of non-violent action inside the situation have been tried and failed. 'Sanctions, many argue, are not worth struggling for because they will cost nations more than they are willing to pay. That is not an argument against the desirability of effective sanctions. It is an argument for beginning a more effective movement in the economically more powerful Western nations, in particular Britain, to make an economic boycott of South Africa politically possible' (p.71). The churches should declare their solidarity with the aims of the revolution in southern Africa, and elsewhere. The Christian Church would then be able both to assist in calculating the cost of building a truly free human society and advise on the way to do it.

The WCC document, entitled 'Violence, Non-violence and the struggle for Social Justice' was presented to the Central Committee in August 1973. It discusses the problem of the Christian when faced with a violent structure, the only way of removing which seems to be by even greater violence. It is recognized that we live in a violent world, and that in some situations Christians find themselves on opposing sides in the conflict. The Gospels seem to indicate that Jesus did not use violence on behalf of the weak and poor against the rich and strong. His rejection of violence may have been situational, it may have been absolute, for all time. In the end the Report comes out most strongly for the pursuit of non-violent but militant challenging action. The classic Christian compromise, over something on which many Christians are just not prepared to be compromised. The Report concludes however with some direct criticism, 'Certainly the fact that some Christians are acting violently for justice and peace, while others are acting non-violently, is a problem; but the greatest problem is that most of those who name Christ as Lord are not consciously acting on the matter at all . . . Christians (must) become wiser and more courageous in translating their commitment to Jesus Christ into specific social and political engagement for social justice' (p.19).

The Report points out that the decision to campaign for the withdrawal of investment can be termed a 'violent' position, it seeks the destruction of the enemy rather than his conversion. We do not accept that, we aim at the creation of a 'peaceful crisis' in South Africa, as Oliver Tambo of the ANC called it, which we believe will bring 'the enemy' to his senses before it is too late. We also believe that 'violent' economic action is one of the very few ways left of influencing apartheid sufficiently to change it before it is too late. If so we must be prepared to pay some of the cost. It may include rejecting the consumption of all South African goods, and persuading others to do likewise, confronting companies who remain in South Africa to profit from the system, taking cuts in salaries or pensions because we will not accept money earned by the exploitation of Africans under apartheid. These are token gestures indeed when faced with the potential suffering of Africans, but owls are wise and far-seeing, while pussycats live only for the moment. Both past and present Presidents of the ANC, Albert Lutuli and Nelson Mandela, have called for international economic boycott, and have said they are prepared to suffer, or to die. Lutuli did die, and Mandela still suffers. And the pussycats still purr over the cream.

7 Chicken or fox?

The argument for withdrawal

NO WONDER the British Council of Churches would not accept officially its 1970 International Affairs Department Report on 'Violence in Southern Africa', urging us as it did to the serious consideration of sanctions and boycotts against white-dominated South Africa. The BCC would then have been even less likely to get financial assistance for an Ecumenical Unit to direct the churches' investments campaign, in fact such radical suggestions might have left it with no financial assistance at all. Why are sanctions and disinvestment regarded with such paranoia by the British churches? As Elisabeth Adler points out in *A Small Beginning,* the likely initial result of the campaign is that a few small companies, or larger companies with comparatively small South African interests, might withdraw, and that a greater number of companies might well re-consider any future planned investment. The Withdrawal Campaign of the Anti-Apartheid Movement stated that two initial steps to be taken by companies to show good faith would be to commit themselves to no more investment, and no more white emigration, to take South African jobs.

But it must not be denied that ultimately the campaign for withdrawal hopes for much more than this. It hopes for a meaningful decision by the multi-national corporations of the western world that South Africa is no longer a place where money can be invested with a good conscience. (It does not offer a profitable alternative to those corporations). Who would be the greatest losers if that were to be the eventual effect of the campaign? The Africans, answer the protagonists of the 'reform' strategy. Not so, says Professor Linnemann of the Free University of Amsterdam. In fact he claims this will 'enhance rather than impair the prospects of improving the socio-economic position of South Africa's coloured population'[1].

How does Linnemann reach this conclusion? He notes first as we have done the importance to South Africa of the inflow of foreign capital and technology, an inflow which keeps up the resulting outflow of industrial goods and manufactured products, as well as some raw materials, to the West. This enables South Africa to carry a loss in her balance of payments, but it will only continue as long as Western capital believes South Africa is a safe and stable system. Foreign investment does of course create job opportunities, agrees Linnemann, but these are directed at two particular groups in the local population, skilled managers and technicians (white), and cheap unskilled labour (black). There is a large gap of opportunities in the middle of the labour force, which of course suits the apartheid system just fine.

---

[1]*Study Encounter,* Vol. X, No. 3, 62. 1973.

What then would be the immediate effect of a halt in investment from abroad? Initially a loss of jobs — for whites and blacks alike — and this would at first have more effect on the black population. However whites will also be hit, and increasingly hard, as it becomes clear there is no overseas market for their high-technology products. There are then two alternatives, either emigration (of both people and capital) or production for the domestic market. The second is the most likely, so that if South Africa can be isolated economically, painful though this may be for the African population at first, the economy will then demand the development of the domestic sector, which in turn will mean higher wages, better opportunities, and increased economic power for blacks. 'It is for these reasons,' says Linnemann, 'that I believe the call for disinvestment (withdrawal) from South Africa should be welcomed by every person who wants to see a genuine improvement of the socio-economic position of the black population in South Africa.'

Professor Linnemann admits that this does not necessarily mean the disappearance of apartheid, but his argument cuts the ground from under the feet of those who protest their concern at the effect of economic boycott and withdrawal on the black African, while continuing to take home their profits under their arm. What such withdrawal would do is to create a new situation, a radical discontinunity, a possibility of peaceful crisis, and peaceful revolution. The time has come for us to respond to the call of Canon Burgess Carr, General Secretary of the All-Africa Council of Churches, who has said, '(We) categorically and forcefully repudiate those protagonists of the reformist faction, whether they are white or black, African or Afrikaaner, related to corporate investment in South Africa. We take the view that the United States and other nations, as well as multinational corporations, must disengage themselves from complicity in the exploitation of black people in southern Africa. This is the only strategy that holds out the prospect for effecting change in southern Africa without recourse to force and armed conflagration'.[2] How much longer are the British churches going to ignore the loud, persistent and radical voices from black South Africa that the path of sacrifice and suffering is the Christian one? So far our gestures of concern and dismay have cost us nothing; the hardest part of tough and sacrificial action will be that others may suffer more than we do. On the question of injustice, exploitation and human misery the British churches should be in Gethsemane. If they are, unfortunately, like the disciples, they are clearly asleep.

Is then the position of withdrawal by companies, or, if they refuse, disinvestment by the churches, that of the chicken or the fox? Are we running away by pulling out, or are we cunningly creating the possibility of radical change in a situation, which is much more the prerogative of the fox? We believe that in the longer term it will be seen to be a far, far wiser

[2] Elizabeth Adler, *A Small Beginning*, p.49.

stance to argue for withdrawal and disinvestment, though as we have said with the latter the retention of a few shares to continue the pressure is not ruled out.

The Christian churches in Britain should come together now, preferably with sister churches from Europe and North America to implement the strategy worked out by the World Council of Churches, on the advice of the African Liberation Movements, as to how a real redistribution of power might take place in southern Africa. It has to be recognized that such fundamental change cannot take place without suffering. We must therefore be prepared to suffer, in terms of popularity or finance, even though it is undoubtedly the Africans who will suffer most. There really is not much cost in standing up publicly in company meetings to request disengagement from southern Africa, in demanding from Christian businessmen and others that they take seriously their moral obligations, in selling all but a token number of shares in profitable companies who will not accept the demands of racial justice and cease South African operations. But we do seem prepared to resort to almost anything rather than pay such limited cost. Is the church now so much a part of the profit-dominated capitalist system that it has lost its grounding in the cross of Christ, and become like the tape-recorder that speaks mechanical messages of hope and joy over the telephone when the 'Phone-in Parson' has long gone home? If this is so, and sadly there seems little current evidence to doubt it, the time may have come when radical Christians should turn their back on the Church, and give their energy to the destruction of capitalism as the system which appears to have totally undermined the integrity of Christianity in the Western Church.

Epilogue

ON ONE occasion a group of church financiers came up to him, saying, 'Teacher, what good thing must we do to inherit eternal life?'

'Good?' he said. 'Why do you ask me about that? Only One is good. But if you wish to enter into Life, keep the commandments.'

'Which commandments?' they asked.

'Do not murder, do not steal; don't be covetous and greedy; remember the Sabbath — and don't cause anyone to work seven days a week for the companies in which you invest. And love your neighbour as yourself.'

The financiers said to him, 'We have done all these, at least we have done our best. Where do we still fall short?'

Looking at them the Teacher loved them all. He answered, 'Go, sell all your investments in companies which shamelessly exploit their employees, destroy human dignity, and support oppression. And if you must invest, do it at maximum benefit for the community, rather than for yourselves.'

At that their faces fell, and they went away sorrowfully, for they had great investments in companies involved in South Africa, and some of the directors were their best friends.

Looking after them the Teacher said, 'You know, it's easier to drive a London bus through a needle's eye than for rich churchmen to enter the Kingdom of God.'